Praise for

ICE
WALKER

"For most of my life, I have read stories of animals, stories that possibly made me who I am. My heroes have been the likes of Ernest Thompson Seton, who was able to get inside the skin of other creatures without anthropomorphizing. James Raffan's *Ice Walker* is a worthy member of that tradition. As he captures the smells, sounds, and feel of the Arctic, we become engaged and travel with Nanu and share her world. We care about her, her cubs, and her environment and end up wanting to protect those all the more. This book is important reading!"

ROBERT BATEMAN, Canadian naturalist, artist, and bestselling author of *Life Sketches* and *Robert Bateman's Canada*

"An unbearable truth shadows every page of this intimate portrait of a female polar bear and her rapidly changing world. Our reliance on fossil fuels has placed us all on thin ice, bears and humans together. James Raffan enlarges our sympathies with this quiet, unsentimental call to fellow-feeling and action."

CANDACE SAVAGE, FRSC, award-winning writer and naturalist

"Stories touch us in ways that no list of facts can. James Raffan proves to be a master storyteller, bringing us an intimate saga of a polar bear's three-year life cycle. Beautifully drawn with scientific accuracy and cultural sensitivity that comprehends the land itself and all its inhabitants, *Ice Walker* gives us a fresh sense of the reality of climate change."

BERT HORWOOD, author and emeritus professor of science education at Queen's University

"This is a great piece of Canadian literature. Raffan's painstakingly simple and stark prose combine with an impressive firsthand knowledge of the landscape and its inhabitants to create a compelling and worrisome story that holds a powerful mirror of accountability up to us and what we are doing to this amazing planet."

GRANT LINNEY, environmentalist, polar educator, and presenter with Al Gore's Climate Reality Project

"Just as a polar bear slips between worlds, from solid ground to sea ice and back again, James Raffan moves effortlessly between the tangible and the imaginative in this strikingly evocative, scientifically rigorous exploration of 'bearness.' In journeying vicariously with a female polar bear through a world in flux, we see that no one and nothing exists in isolation, especially in the far north. Failing to recognize this reality more broadly will only accelerate our undoing. *Ice Walker*, then, is an act of defiance and hope. This is nature writing at its most intimate, compassionate, and exhilarating pitch."

KATE HARRIS, award-winning and bestselling author of *Land of Lost Borders*

Also by
James Raffan

—

ICE WALKER

A Polar Bear's Journey through the Fragile Arctic

—

JAMES RAFFAN

Phyllis Bruce Editions
SIMON & SCHUSTER CANADA
New York   London   Toronto   Sydney   New Delhi

SIMON &
SCHUSTER
CANADA

Simon & Schuster Canada
A Division of Simon & Schuster, Inc.
166 King Street East, Suite 300
Toronto, Ontario M5A 1J3

Phyllis Bruce Editions, published by Simon & Schuster Canada

This Simon & Schuster Canada edition September 2020

SIMON & SCHUSTER CANADA and colophon are
trademarks of Simon & Schuster, Inc.

For information about special discounts for bulk purchases,
please contact Simon & Schuster Special Sales at 1-800-268-3216
or CustomerService@simonandschuster.ca.

Interior design by Lewelin Polanco

Manufactured in the United States of America

1 3 5 7 9 10 8 6 4 2

Library and Archives Canada Cataloguing in Publication

Title: Ice walker / James Raffan.
Names: Raffan, James, author.
Description: Simon & Schuster Canada edition.
Identifiers: Canadiana 20200164287 | ISBN 9781501155369 (hardcover)
Subjects: LCSH: Polar bear—Effect of global warming on—
Hudson Bay. | LCSH: Polar bear—Climatic factors—
Hudson Bay. | LCSH: Global warming—Hudson Bay. |
LCSH: Climatic changes—Hudson Bay. |
LCSH: Global temperature changes—Environmental aspects—Hudson Bay.
Classification: LCC QL737.C27 R34 2020 | DDC 599.786—dc23
ISBN 978-1-5011-5536-9
ISBN 978-1-5011-5538-3 (ebook)

To Huxley, wherever you are.

Contents

CONTENTS

A woman had a miscarriage and ran away from her family. As she ran, she came to a house. In the passage lay the skins of bears.

She went in. The inhabitants turned out to be bears in human shape.

But she stayed with them. The big bear caught seals for them. He pulled on his skin and went out, often remaining away for some time, but always eventually bringing something home.

One day, the woman who had run away took a fancy to see her relations and wanted to go home. Then the mother bear spoke. "Do not talk about us when you get back to men," she said. She was afraid that her two young ones might be killed by men.

So the woman went home, and a great desire came over her. And one day, as she sat caressing her husband, she whispered in his ear, "I have seen bears."

Many sledges drove out, and when the mother bear saw them coming toward their house, she had great compassion on her young ones and bit them to death. She did not wish them to fall into the power of men.

Then she rushed out to look for the woman who had deceived them. She broke into the house where the woman was and bit her to death. When she came out again, the dogs closed up a circle around her and rushed upon her.

The bear defended herself, but suddenly she and the dogs all became luminous and rose into the sky as stars. And those are what they call Qilugtûsat—they who are like a flock of barking dogs after a bear.

Since then, Inuit have been cautious about bears, for they hear what people say.

—Adapted from an Inuit story told by Greenlandic Inuk Aisivak to explorer Knud Rasmussen in his book *The People of the Polar North*, 1908

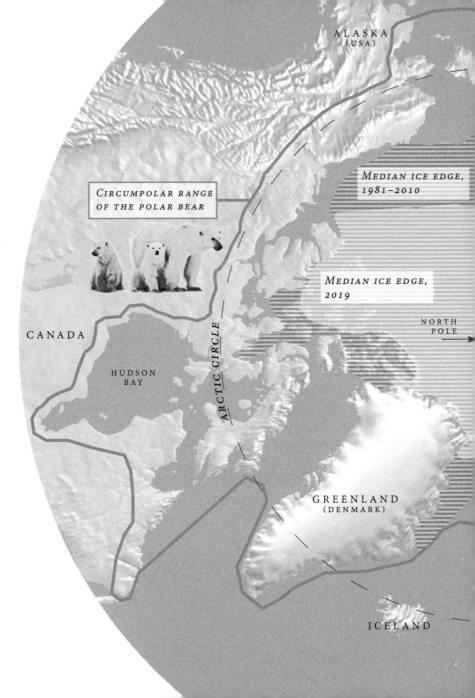

ALASKA
(USA)

Median ice edge,
1981–2010

Circumpolar range
of the polar bear

Median ice edge,
2019

NORTH
POLE

CANADA

HUDSON
BAY

ARCTIC CIRCLE

GREENLAND
(DENMARK)

ICELAND

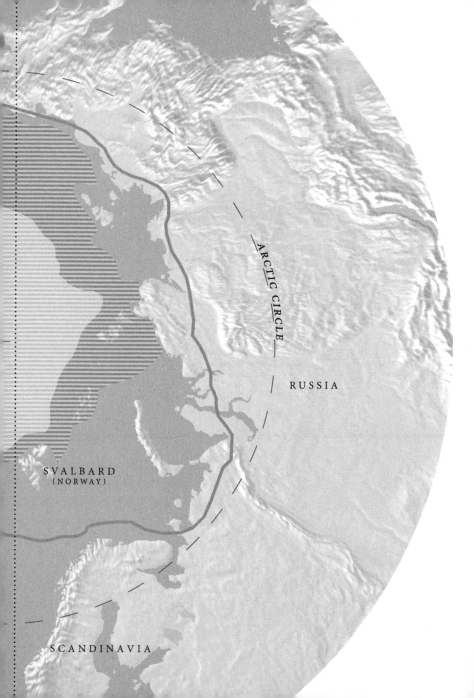

magine you are in the International Space Station, curving over northern North America. From the heavens, Hudson Bay looks like an enormous paw print on the torso of the continent, a massive beating heart drawing lifeblood from a vast network of lakes and rivers that drain nearly 1.5 million square miles of what is now the United States and Canada. At the estuaries of all the great rivers that flow into the bay, freshwater and seawater mix and begin to swirl in a great counterclockwise gyre that freezes and thaws, contracts and releases, as the earth makes its way around the sun.

Daily tides impelled by the moon, swayed by movement of earth around the sun, pulse the big bay in sinus rhythm. In the spring, great floes of ice pump rhythmically through Hudson Strait into the Labrador Current and on into global oceanic circulation. Mists rising off those same waters are energized by the sun. They rise and swirl in the atmosphere, eventually returning to earth as rain or snow on the high ground, where the cycle is renewed.

Now imagine, in the middle of all that pulsing, renewing energy, one seven-year-old female polar bear, striding into an uncertain future, as another thirty-six months in the Arctic unfold.

In Canada, the Cree, to the south, call her Wabusk. The Inuit, to the north, call her Nanuq or Pihoqahiak, the Ever Wandering One. And because these iconic white carnivores occupy the entire circumpolar world, people throughout the region know her as well. The Sami in Scandinavia and western Russia call her God's Dog, never mentioning her name. In Greenland, she is Tornassuk, the master of helping spirits. Throughout the Arctic she has other names: the Old Man/Woman in a Fur Coat; Sea Bear; Ice Bear; Ah-tik-tok (the One Who Goes Down to the Sea); the Lady of the Arctic; White Sea Deer; or even Farmer, by whalers who mocked her pigeon-toed gait. Science calls her *Ursus maritimus*, meaning "sea bear" in Latin. Common usage terms her a polar bear. Whatever her name, this is home. And home is changing.

The tracks she is making, as she walks on a midwinter day, are on a trail that leads back more than a hundred and fifty thousand years. There are almost no terrestrial fossil records of polar bears, because most of them have lived and died on or over water. She is a bear of the sea, but she is a direct descendant of land bears. Emerging DNA evidence and biogeographical analysis indicate that Siberia is the most likely place where polar bears first emerged. Whether it was competition for limited resources or evolutionary pressure that forced them to explore new habitats, brown bears moved off the land and onto the Arctic ice all those years ago.

On the ice, lighter-colored bears proved more successful hunters of seal than darker-colored bears. Bears with longer canine teeth, and with a longer gap back to their molars, could hunt seals more efficiently because their bite was more lethal. Bears with thicker coats, furrier paws, and smaller noses and ears also did better in the cold. And a unique ability to metabolize a diet of more fat than protein allowed them to out-compete their darker, terrestrial cousins.

Seal fat is the perfect food for polar bears. It provides the maximum benefit for the minimum effort, when it comes to hunting. Science tells us that burning anything creates carbon dioxide and water. Because polar bears live in an environment where liquid freshwater is nonexistent for much of the year, they benefit from the interior production of water as part of the process of metabolizing the energy-rich seal fat. Our bear, then, is perfectly adapted to a life on the ice.

How many polar bears are there today? By combining historical data with a few decades of systematic censusing, scientists agree that today there might be something like twenty-five thousand polar bears in nineteen separate populations distributed along the coasts of Greenland, Svalbard, Norway, Russia, Alaska, and Canada. The western Hudson Bay population is estimated to be about six thousand bears, allowing an average of more than seventy-seven square miles per individual bear. Which means our bear will often travel alone in a vast landscape of ice and snow.

As evolutionary luck would have it, another mammal also

began its evolution into its current expression about two hundred thousand years ago. Like the bear, *Homo sapiens* also eventually moved from the land of the northern forest onto the ice of the Arctic, perhaps ten thousand years ago, in search of food or opportunity, or to avoid conflict—whatever the cause, the first human dwellers of the northern ice were adapted spectacularly to life there. These first human inhabitants of the ice, those who became the modern Inuit, would never have been able to move beyond the boreal forest, with its ready supply of firewood and food, unless they were able to hunt seals. On land, the trees were a source of fuel for cooking and warmth; on ice, the fat of sea mammals—seals, principally—fired their flames, allowing them to exist above the tree line. It was the hunt for this precious source of energy for their cooking lamps, or "qulliq," that connected early Inuit to the other large fuel-hungry predator in this realm, the polar bear.

Perhaps it was the ferocity and majesty of the bear that garnered both fear and respect as it competed for seals, or maybe there was something in the bear's eerie resemblance to a human being when skinned. Whatever it was, through predator–prey relationships, competition for seals as a food source, stories, myths or the unexplainable, bears became intertwined with early human experience on the sea ice of the circumpolar world. The story told to explorer Knud Rasmussen by Greenlandic Inuk Aisivak, about the woman who lived with bears after having a miscarriage, is but one of an international multicultural trove of tales, legends and lore celebrating the age-old relationship between polar bears and Arctic peoples.

Since this early time, polar bears and polar peoples have been cohabiting one of the most challenging and unforgiving habitats on earth. For as much as polar bears have evolved to live in the icescapes of the circumpolar Arctic, so, too, have the northern peoples, in large part because of the seal. And it is this triad of bear, hunter, and seal—and the ice on which they live—that is central to the survival of the Arctic world. They all have the right to thrive and to be cold.

Today, we face daily warnings that a human-caused warming of the climate is melting ice and threatening life, particularly in the polar regions. In most instances, we are shown images and stories of beleaguered polar bears struggling to survive on disappearing ice or being harvested for food or sport. We hear much less about the people of the north, most of whom, like the bears, also rely on an intimate and existential relationship with ice for a significant part of the year. Both have lessons to teach us.

The story that follows has its genesis in my belief that the intertwining worlds of northern bears and northern peoples offer deep wisdom that the rest of us could use to adjust our behavior in response to climate change. In spite of unanimity in the scientific community about its existence and graphic evidence of its accelerating effects on our lives through flooding, sea level rise, forest fires, and increased catastrophic weather events around the world, very little of what we see and hear seems to translate into action.

Should we begin to appreciate fully the global changes wrought by human appetites, we might begin to understand that the threats to polar bears are also profound threats to us. Only then will we have the ability to create a shift in perspective from which real solutions can be forged.

one
Circling

ᐊᏉᕠᓂ ᐱᑉ

Miscarriage Moon

FEBRUARY

—

Seven-year-old Nanurjuk, "the bear-spirited one," is hunting for seals on Hudson Bay in Canada's Arctic on a frosty day in February. The temperature on the ice is −37°C. The temperature of the blood circulating through arteries and veins of her massive feet is around +37°C. Exposed human flesh at this temperature freezes in minutes. And yet in the half inch between the surface of the snow and the inside of her feet, there is a temperature difference of 74 degrees. Bumps or papillae in her hair-covered soles are a two-way communication system, sensing differences in ice texture and temperature. Through skin glands, she sends signals to anyone who will cross her track with the right sensory equipment. The message today is that she is healthy and coming into season.

Behind her, an Arctic fox, moving like white wind on the shadowed snow, follows from a distance, in the hope of scraps from the hunt. Like a wolf, the fox walks more on her toes. The polar bear, as all bears do, steps forward onto her heels, leaving full round footprints wherever she goes. A bigger foot area produces a snowshoe effect in deep snow, exerting less pressure on thin ice. Her hind feet step perfectly into the prints of her front feet, saving the energy she would need to expend to break track with all four feet in deep snow. The impression she leaves on this trail she's making is that she is on just two legs, upright like a woman.

She stops and sniffs the frigid air, with almost no vapor trail from her mouth or nose. In a frozen world where liquid freshwater for drinking is absent, she draws on metabolic water created by the burning of seal fat, her main food source. The outside air is desert dry, but the air in her lungs is humid. Somehow she is able to conserve moisture and stay sufficiently hydrated, even when running or exerting herself physically in the hunt, when a human would soon die from winter dehydration. Every one of these adaptations is a marvel that has taken untold generations to evolve. These are not physiological changes that can respond to seasonal or even annual environmental shifts.

Nanu has fared better this winter than last, when she mated successfully for the first time, but without sufficient energy stores to see her pregnancy through to live births. Toward the end of that pregnancy, her first, as she waited alone in the quiet and relative safety of her den, under spruce roots in the bank of a stream far inland, she felt the movement deep within her, but then it stopped. When the contractions came, the two cubs were stillborn. There was nothing to be done but head back to the winter ice to start again.

This year, the hunting has been better. Still, with a hunting success rate of about one seal in twenty tries, she must work hard to kill enough for the calories she needs. Once every week or ten days, with constant roaming, vigilance, stealth and a bit of luck, she has scored adult ringed and bearded seals who have offered a generous coating of blubber. Most times, she leaves the meat, bone and viscera for the fox, her constant companion, and for the ravens who, no matter what the weather or how low the temperature may be, will show up and comment on her kills. Sometimes, when they tiptoe too close to the edge of her patience, she lunges, and they cackle.

In her first winter, as she was learning about the ice and the hunt with her mother, Nanu experienced a stillness of winter ice she has not seen since. Back then, seven years ago, the bay surface froze thick and deep. When the temperature would rise or fall by a few degrees, enough to make the ice expand or contract, the peace would be broken with cannon booms of cracks forming. The booms would echo off low clouds or bounce off pressure ridges. Otherwise, her world was silent.

In the blue blackness of winter's coldest nights, cracks or "leads" where seals might breathe were few and far between. Prey moved elsewhere, perhaps to the floe edge in the deepest waters in the middle of the bay. Resting when her cubs were tired, nursing all the while, her mother did her best to provide for Nanu and her brother. Now, if this is the year for the birth cycle to continue, she will be called upon to do the same, should she become pregnant again.

On this late February day, the ice is talkative, moved by

wind and current and murmuring constantly with voices that sound old and crotchety at one moment, young and squeaky at another, like summer gulls. Pressure ridges form along the cracks, rising like mini mountain ranges and snaking toward the sky. At other times, the grinding of ice on ice creates keels that push down into the water, inverted mountain ranges that create rich habitats for plankton, krill, fish and ultimately seals, who make their way into Nanu's diet—when she gets lucky.

Clambering up and down and over these ridges takes energy, but the reward for working fractured ice is success in the hunt. And when it snows, as it seems to be doing more now than she remembers from the early days, the mountain ridges provide places for the winds to eddy and drifts to form, places for unfettered sleeps or for rolling to clean her face and fur after eating. When Nanu naps, she knows these nooks will keep her away from view and prevent her scent from being unnecessarily broadcast downwind. Marauding big male bears are less of a risk when there are places to hide, ice panels to break the wind and divert her scent, complicate her trail, and lengthen her time for reaction.

Today, the active ice makes it difficult to discern what might be a seal and what might be just moving ice. But visual cues are only part of the hunt. She has other sensory resources at her disposal. With the sensitivity of those amazing feet, she can feel vibrations in the ice. Sometimes, these are from the movement of the ice itself, other times, from seals scratching and scraping as they tend their breathing holes. She can also sense vibrations with her ears, which are sensitive to even the subtlest of movements. And, happily, there is always the smell of seal, especially at this time of year, when the ringed seals and the bigger bearded seals are whelping the year's crop of young. Because Nanu does the bulk of her winter foraging under star-bright skies, the more sensory cues she has, the better.

With a gamboling offhand walk, her head swinging rhythmically from side to side, sniffing the ice, testing the air for more than an hour, Nanu has been following tendrils of seal smell that add purpose to her gait the stronger they get. Her sense of smell is so finely tuned that when she crosses a vapor trail like this one, she can sense the direction it is coming from and be assured that she is moving toward the prey. Today, without question, there is seal on the wind.

Experience has taught Nanu that seals are formidable in their ability to avoid capture. They, too, can differentiate sounds underwater almost as well as they do in air. So Nanu takes care to ensure that she gets the upper hand. Despite her considerable size and mass, she places each foot deliberately to avoid percussive pressure on the ice or any cracking of surface crystals, which might betray her intentions to nearby prey.

She stops between two bus-sized chunks of ice and lets her belly rest on the cool surface beside an almost imperceptible dome in the surface of the new snow. This is an aglu, a breathing hole for seals. She quiets her own breathing and tips her head, listening. The seal smell has been getting stronger as she draws closer to this exact point. She waits for the familiar compression of air when the seal's face breaks the surface of the water in the aglu. Immediately following that will be a swoosh of water as the seal pulls itself up into its den under the snow. She waits in silence.

With luck, this seal will be nursing a pup—a whitecoat—who will be unable to enter the water just yet. She listens.

Nothing. There is a faint smell of blood, a good sign. She listens again to see if she can hear the murmur of a nursing mother. Nothing. She knows the challenge here is to catch the mother, who will provide a much more satisfying meal than the pup. Again she waits, at the air hole, completely still.

At last, her whiskers sense the sonic puff of air. Slowly, reflexively, she coils herself back onto her haunches, pulling her hind legs under her and allowing her forelegs to extend so that her massive shoulders and chest are as high off the snow as possible. And then, in an explosion of energy, cold air, and flying snow, she rises up and crashes down, punching through the new snow and the crusted dome of the lair onto the unsuspecting adult seal. She can feel her grasping claws sink into the soft belly of the seal as it turns to dive back into the safety of the water, and then with strength and precision, she plunges her head through the hole, her curved canine teeth penetrating and crushing the soft skull of the seal, killing it instantly.

Nanu jams her feet onto the floor of the aglu, snatches the seal and flings it out onto the surface of the ice, where blood belches into the new snow. She grabs the whitecoat, too, and does the same, although it is of much less interest as food now that the adult has been caught.

Wasting no time, she rolls her warm prize onto its side and, with razor-sharp incisors, cuts and yanks back the drying gray pelt, devouring mouthfuls of blubber as she goes. Before she is finished, she has used those same front teeth to flense all of the available fat from both the skin and the musculature of the seal as quickly as possible. The fractured ice hides her from other bears who might find their way to this kill, but its smell is already telegraphing across the ice. She must eat from this seal before anyone else decides to join the feast.

Afterward, as she dozes, Nanu hears the faraway whine of something in the distance. Someone else is hunting on the ice. In time, acrid vapors will be coming her way on the wind. But before she can make anything more of that sound, a dog barks, then several sharp sounds reverberate. Because this is something that has been with her for her entire life and in the lives of her parents and grandparents, she knows there is another predator on the ice, the only one that is a real threat, but it is far away. The whine is fading now. With night coming, she can sleep without fear.

Hours later, Nanu rouses briefly to the sound of an Arctic fox picking away at the remains of her kill, but she dozes off again immediately, for this is not a threat. In fact, had the fox not shown up, particularly on a spectacular winter night like this, it might have been a sign that all was not well.

While she sleeps, Nanu's remarkable digestive system goes to work immediately, breaking down the fat into its constituent parts, channeling trace nutrients and other minerals and compounds where they need to go, and converting the rest of the seal tissue into available energy that will be stored elsewhere. If this next reproductive round is to be successful, she will need every bit she can store. She needs to be as healthy as she can because her life is about to change.

Having recovered from her stillbirth experience barely five months earlier, her body is readying itself for another pregnancy. Amazingly, news of all of this—her general health, her weight, and her sexual readiness—is being published in every big round track she makes. Glands on the soles of her feet continue to leave olfactory messages for the males who follow her, signaling that she is healthy and coming into season.

—

Nanu senses the presence of other bears long before she actually sees them. There are three suitors in total.

First, the massive scarred old boar walking with a powerful, confident gait. Nineteen years of life on the ice and the odd tussle with a canny walrus have left him hairless in places and noticeably battle worn.

Next in line, keeping a healthy distance from the scarred old boar, is a ten-year-old handsome male. A combination of size, strength, tactics, and respect for bigger, stronger males has kept him in good form. He has almost no scars at all, at least none that are visible. He jumps confidently from ridge to ridge of ice, never losing his balance.

Last in line is a six-year-old youthful boar, who is healthy and strong but less mature. What is distinctive about him is his tail, a little longer than the others', and his middle toe, noticeably longer as well.

Each bear, in his own time and on his own schedule, has been following her tracks. Hunting, yes, but always picking up her trail again, using it as a marker. And although hunting is never better than it is right now under this February miscarriage moon, the male drive to mate eclipses all. Soon it will overshadow even the drive to eat, to nourish powerful male bodies.

After the three bears comes the fox, who can smell Nanu's tracks and knows what this parade is all about. With all this bearness on the move, there will be lots to eat in the foreseeable future. She is there but not there, moving quickly when she has to, then curling up like a shadow in the mist when need be.

Disconnected from one another but following the same instincts, the three male bears move in a great circle that is being drawn on the ice of Hudson Bay by Nanu. The scent in her tracks and in the occasional places where she urinates gets stronger by degrees, indicating that she is reaching the point where she might be receptive.

The sun moves higher in the sky, and with each passing day, its heat and the general warming of the atmosphere will start to soften and break up the ice. The heart of North America is alive and readying to contract and flush out this year's fractured ice through Hudson Strait and into global oceanic circulation, where, as the ice moves into warmer waters, it will eventually disintegrate. Farther north, where multiyear ice still exists, things are less transient. But here on Hudson Bay, as is the case along the circumpolar coastlines in Svalbard, Norway; Russia; Alaska; and continental North America, where ice never lasts any longer than one season, everything is in flux. This parade of bears is happening on ice that is moving, literally, under their feet.

Nanu is wary because she knows that big males might just as easily attack her as catch a seal and share it. But another instinct compels her to see who is following her, and to assess whether or not he will make a worthy suitor.

Torn by these inclinations, Nanu does what bears instinctively know how to do. She plots her position in space and time, as a sailor might do on the ocean using the stars—who knows?—to determine a direction of travel. Then she continues the endless search for her next meal, always bearing a little bit to the right in her steps. As a result, her tracks trace a giant circle, perhaps three miles in radius, on her late-winter journey that will bring her back to her own track of days earlier. Here, when the circle is complete, she encounters the tracks of three other bears. Big tracks. Boar tracks. Tracks that speak to Nanu of readiness.

two
Dancing

ᒪ^ᐊᓅᑦ

Eggs Moon

JUNE

—

As the last gossamer blues of the Arctic night leach from the sky in the latter days of May, the three hopeful males follow Nanu at varying distances. Nanu's shadow circles her in a clockwise direction: In the morning, it is long and walking to her left. As the day progresses, it contracts and moves ahead of her. By afternoon, it is beside her to the right, and by midnight, as the sun moves through the north, it follows her from behind. Mirroring the passage of solar time is an internal clock that has been ticking, too—this one sending signals that she is readying to mate.

She continues to seek leads and cracks in the ice where the hunting will be good. Regardless of suitors, she must hunt to survive. Still, in every step, she is determined to see who is following. She naps after eating, keeping one eye open for possible visitors. The fox joins her, as do the ravens, spinning out of clear spring skies now full of chattering geese and other migrants heading north to their summer nesting grounds.

Still out of sight, her suitors are hunting, too, but with less dedication. The handsome ten-year-old gets lucky with a young bearded seal cow whose pup had strayed farther than she should have from water access. The seal decides to nurse alongside a pressure ridge. Calculating the breeze, and showing surprising stealth given his mammoth size, he drops down on them from above. Only the young one gets away.

When the scarred old boar catches wind of this kill, he momentarily deviates from Nanu's scent. When he shows up at the feeding site, the ten-year-old, perhaps sensing the battles yet to come, departs immediately, leaving the older bear to eat. The younger bear takes advantage of the situation and presses on after Nanu.

The handsome ten-year-old is first to catch up with her. She is sleeping on an open plain of smooth ice. He approaches to within a hundred yards or so and sits down, purposely upwind from her. He wants her to know he is there. It isn't long before she opens her eyes and sits up as well. Two healthy white bears face one another on the crystalline spring ice.

The handsome ten-year-old makes the first move. He gets up and takes a few tentative steps toward Nanu, who simply watches before getting up herself. She exposes her left side to him and walks a line that is ninety degrees to his. Nanu's move forces the young boar to alter his course. She stops. He stops. And then, gingerly, he approaches her from the back and sniffs. With indifference, she rises and walks on, as if he is not there at all.

And so it continues for several hours, until the full-bellied old boar lumbers into view. Without a moment's hesitation, he charges across the ice. Nanu saunters along, seemingly oblivious to the opening moves in what will be nearly a week of battles for her favors.

The old boar's first move, however, is not to engage the younger bear. Instead, he turns and starts moving toward Nanu, as if it is a forgone conclusion that she is his, uncontested. In doing so, he has provided the young boar with a difficult choice: he can either walk away, having now seen the prize and the competition, or he can announce his intentions to the old boar by also moving toward the female.

The contest is on. The two males close in on each other, swinging their heads back and forth and growling under their breath. Nanu lies down on the ice, facing away from the two boars. Now on their hind feet, like prizefighters coming fresh out of their respective corners, they collide with a gnashing of spit and teeth. Spreading their forepaws in the air as if to show off their impressive reach and broad chests, mouths open, they engage. The old boar bites hard on the young boar's neck and the two of them knuckle down to the snow. The young boar scrambles back to regroup.

In terms of sheer mass, the old bear has the advantage. But the younger bear is equally tall, though leaner, and has a similar reach. Again they approach on hind legs. The younger bear still appears not to understand just how serious this skirmish might be. With forepaws flailing, he snaps at the older bear's face and neck. But when the old bear plants his forepaws on his opponent's shoulders, he is forced to step back. He regroups, then charges. But the old bear is ready for him and savagely bites through the skin of his ruff, drawing blood.

The injury brings the young bear back to the fight with renewed vigor. He bats the old bear's face and shoulders, raking a nasty scar he has found on his opponent's left shoulder with his younger, sharper claws.

Through all this, Nanu is bathing, licking the backs of her paws. Her scent fills the arena, urging the males on.

It doesn't take more than a few minutes for both boars to heat up, tire and retreat to a safe distance from each other. The sparring continues only when one of them makes a move toward the female. At the warmest part of the day, everyone, including Nanu, naps as the temperature of the air around these super-insulated mammals rises temporarily above freezing.

During one of these rests, the third boar creeps to within fifty yards of Nanu. The old boar instantly charges the newcomer with a vengeance. Within seconds he has drawn blood on his shoulder and face. The third boar retreats as the old boar continues to lunge toward him, pushing him back to a respectable distance.

The old boar now moves quickly toward Nanu. She gets up from where she is sitting and starts to amble up an inclined ice plane toward a towering pressure ridge that has not yet bent to the strengthening spring sun. This time, she allows him to get close beside her as they walk. They stop and, one at a time, take turns sniffing the other. She licks a couple of the places where his old scars have split and leaked a little blood. He hangs his head over her back from the side and drapes one paw on her rump. She walks on. By the time the sun is back again in the north, they are sleeping together in a heap in a secluded nook in the ridge.

By morning, the young boar is back on the scene, moving quickly toward the pair. The old boar wheels, becoming a snorting, charging opponent. This sow is his and no one else's. The intruder retreats, this time for good.

Now Nanu really is his, at least for now. All the old boar has to do is to protect his right to be at her side, and remain patient.

Under the golden glow of what is now twenty-four-hour daylight, the open leads and old kill sites are now alive with the fritter and flash of returning snow buntings. The ice darkens as it melts, but candling formations of the melting process catch and reflect light back into the sky that one rarely sees in the depths of winter. The two bears make a striking duo. Their coats are at their thickest and most luxuriant. His coat is slightly darker (and bloodstained where the recent jousting has opened small wounds) and more golden. Hers is more blue-white, like the midday snow. When they lie together, his claws are easily lost in the thickness of her fur, as are hers in his.

Eventually she allows him a couple of test mounts, where she momentarily stands completely still. He rises, brings his forequarters over her and rocks his main weight from his hind legs to her back. Then, as if slightly flustered by what has just happened, she turns, rolls and shrugs him off. By and by she stands again, and eventually braces herself to take the weight of his massive shoulders onto her frame and he finds the essential connection.

During the previous weeks of chase and courtship, their reproductive systems have readied themselves for this moment. But only the physical stimulation of her loins will provide the trigger for eggs to be released.

Finally, as Nanu stands, the old boar rises to the occasion. As she moves suddenly to steady herself under the sheer force of his weight on her back, at the actual point of connection his penis bone or "baculum" snaps and the old boar withdraws in pain. She is left with a fertilization process that is started but very much incomplete. He tries again but retires quickly.

Nanu walks on for a time, turns and looks at him, lies down, and looks again at her would-be suitor from a distance. He walks toward her for a few steps, lies down, and stays near for a few more hours. Eventually, he turns and limps away until his movement is swallowed by the glare of the sun. With no male immediately present and interested in mating, she does what she has always done. She lifts her head to assess what threads of seal are in the wind and moves on.

With the mating dance now interrupted, the handsome ten-year-old somehow senses the changing circumstances and circles back. After some initial uncertainty, Nanu eventually allows him access and a new courtship begins. By the time other males come anywhere near, Nanu and her new suitor have had sufficient time over several days to consummate a connection that is as old as time. History written in their respective genes will be expressed in a new generation of polar bears, which the newcomer will likely never see. They part again as perfect strangers.

—

And yet the new miracle begins. Each of one or two fertilized cells in Nanu's uterus divides and become two. Two cells become four cells, which double to eight cells, then sixteen, thirty-two and sixty-four, until a ball of one hundred and twenty-eight cells is created. At this point the process of cell division stops. This conceptus then stays within her, where it will be nourished, protected and incubated at exactly the right temperature, until the fall, if all goes well. Between now and then, however, there is much to be done in the increasingly perilous world of our polar bear.

three
Nesting

ᓯᑉᕆᓂᖅᕕᖕᒃ ᓯᖕᓂᖅᐳᑦ ᐊᓕᐄ

Thin Hair Moon

JULY

—

Nanu's prime directive now is to build sufficient energy reserves to see her through as much as eight months of fasting that will begin the moment she leaves the ice. And although she has yet to bring live cubs into this changing world, her instincts tell her that she is feeding not just one life, but two or three. Her body knows how to draw sparingly from its own resources, but there is a fine line between enough food for all and basic sustenance.

With her walks the memory. Last year, she left the ice in June without sufficient fat to see her through to a successful delivery. She must repeat her mother's success in hunting and providing an abundant supply of nutritious milk for the newborn. In her first season on the ice as a cub, she and her mother and brother were on the ice well into July. Her mother was in good shape after her long pregnancy. That is exactly what Nanu needs to accomplish, although the season seems to be getting shorter and less predictable every year.

After losing her cubs on land, in her first den, this past winter, Nanu had come back onto the ice at 420 pounds, which is well below her ideal weight of 550 pounds—or 600 pounds, in a perfect world. With almost no insulating fat left on her body, she looked gaunt and more humanlike than ever. While she waited with the other bears to return to the ice, she had picked at kelp and grasses and had even surprised and caught a flightless molting goose. But none of that fodder had the kind of calories and nutrition that she craved. The systems of her body were stressed by near starvation.

When she finally did get on the ice and collapsed on the remains of a seal that another bear had harvested, she could feel her body taking every morsel of those bites of mostly meat, not fat, savoring them and putting them to work in the slow process of rebuilding a healthy body. Still, it was some weeks before the dip between her shoulders and the thickness of her waist began to round out. As the deep cold of the darkest time of the year settled in, she was back up to 500 pounds and all of her faculties were functioning as they should, including her maternal processes.

The problems of her previous pregnancy are behind her now. She has done well with her hunting, particularly since the mating hiatus. The seals have started whelping again. Even the fox is looking more robust than usual, and she knows this because when she sleeps she senses her presence, often within view. And although the fox is usually a few steps behind her as she investigates vapor trails, occasionally she will be drawn to hunting sites because the fox has found them first. She often knows where the fox is because one of the ravens will be cruising high above. It is never difficult, even in the dark, to find the fox even when the raven is somewhere else, because of the particular pungency of her pee spots, like markers on the trails, which lead to new hunting possibilities. The three of them coexist in a strange way, depending on one another.

Still, Nanu is far from where she needs to be in terms of weight, if she is to do what it is she is destined to do in the coming months. The fertilized eggs within her must reside in a stronger body if they are going to develop to term and turn into healthy offspring. The challenge is to work as hard as she possibly can, using every faculty at her disposal—and some luck—to build her reserves. The increasingly unpredictable part of her life equation is how long the ice will last. More ice, more seal hunting. More hunting, more success, more fat on her body when she comes ashore.

But it is always a race against time. Nanu's chances to eat well melt in the spring sunshine. Ice and leads forming here and there slowly reduce a vast world of ice over water to a sea of broken ice that is battered by winds and currents in the bay. With ice now fractured into floes, deep-water keels float to the surface and giant pressure ridges collapse. Crystals in surface floes give way to long thin ice candles that sound like wind chimes when swept by the breeze. Nanu's world becomes a symphony of snapping ice, migrating birds, bawling young seals, and hunting two-legs who might one day have her heart in their crosshairs.

With the breakup of the ice, Nanu must exchange the economy of stationary hunting for stealth hunting, which is more energy-intensive but much less effective, as seals can surface almost anywhere. As generalist eaters, seals are free to fish for cod or sculpin or to cruise the ocean bottom for shrimps, crabs or clams, wherever they like without being tied to a particular breathing hole or series of holes in the hard winter ice. Mothers can nurse in the water but often prefer to feed their growing young, and to sleep, sprawled out on the moving ice pans. Stealth hunting is best when the ice covers most of the bay's surface, but if the ice covers less than 30 percent of the water's surface, hunting success drops precipitously. Today, all things considered, hunting conditions are ideal. Nanu can easily make her way across the pack ice on foot, jumping from pan to pan, but she can also swim comfortably in the water. Patience is always key to eating well. She knows how to circle slowly downwind and to choose carefully when and how to approach for the kill.

Nanu spies a sleeping mother seal and pup, a pair of dark spots on distance ice. She slips into the water and navigates with only her head barely visible between floes. Sometimes, she just stops and floats, the surface of the water drawing a line from the corner of her mouth to just below her ear. To get to her prey, she must take a circuitous route, but her sense of direction is sure. When she is two hundred yards from the sleeping seal, she takes one last long inhalation and slips beneath the surface of the water.

With her front feet paddling exactly as they do when she is swimming on the surface, her back feet trailing behind for steering, she continues the last part of her journey toward her quarry skimming just below the broken ice. When she was thinner, she was not buoyant enough to keep much more than her nose above the water when she swam. But now, at over 660 pounds, her growing fat layer is like a life preserver. It is difficult to keep below the water's surface. Light beams through the leads between ice pans and shimmers on the feather-fur that trails from her busy limbs.

Nanu pulls herself deeper into the blue waters of the bay just prior to reaching the spot where she knows the seal is basking. Gathering her limbs and tumbling to an upright position in the water, she reaches up with her forepaws and accelerates like a great white rocket toward the light. Reaching the surface, she explodes onto the ice. Before the seal has time to fathom what is happening, its skull is crushed. The whitecoat escapes. Nanu flings the bleeding adult onto a bigger ice pan nearby, where the final feast of the season begins.

—

A perfectly adapted amphibious creature of water and ice, Nanu delays her return to shore as long as she possibly can, knowing that the longer she stays where the seals stay, the more chance she has of one more kill before the long summer fast. When a spring storm of whistling warm winds and rain dissipates the ice, making it more or less disappear overnight, she is swimming again, riding the tide shoreward.

She has done well. When her paddling front feet touch the red mud of the foreshore flats and her steering back feet reach down to take up her weight in the warm coastal air, fifty-five miles south of Churchill, Manitoba, on the western shore of Hudson Bay, she weighs nearly 700 pounds. She's almost plump compared to the size she was when she walked onto the ice just eight months before. The essential part of the body mass she is bringing ashore is the makings of two new cubs, tucked deep within her belly. This must be the focus of everything she will do for the foreseeable future.

In locations where ice persists year round, Nanu's contemporaries in other polar bear populations around the circumpolar world den on the ice. However, as that area diminishes year by year, heading for land on which to wait out the summer is the only option left. Whether on ice or on land, in Svalbard, Siberia, Alaska or Canada, bears are cohabiting their ranges with two-legged creatures. These are the distinctive northern peoples, each with their own polar bear traditions and habits, mythologies and understandings. By far the majority in that circumpolar cultural realm are the Inuktitut-speaking people, principally the Inuit, who live above the tree line in a geographic swath from the Russian Far East across North America to Greenland.

South of the tree line, polar bear peoples include two other linguistic groups: the Dene, like the Gwich'in, who live more to the north and west of northern North America; and the Cree, who live along the forest more to the center and east of the Athabascan-speaking Dene peoples. The grand oval of Nanu's world in southwestern Hudson Bay intersects with the Dene and Inuit territory in the western part of that range and with the Cree principally in the easterly part of her world. The main community in the Dene/Inuit part of Nanu's world is Churchill, Manitoba. And, to the east, the main community is the Swampy Cree village of Waśaho Ininiwak or Fort Severn First Nation.

The look and smell and feel of the place where Nanu comes ashore is familiar. That she has stood at that exact spot on the Hudson Bay shore is unlikely, though. But the pattern walked by her mother and grandmother before her is still the same, a time onshore to see the summer through, then a gradual turning north with the shortening of days to meet winter working its way south from the pole. The position of the shoreline relative to the sun, the distant vapors of Churchill to the north, the high-pitched sounds of squabbling geese, the squawks of gulls and shorebirds bickering for nesting, even the faint thump-thump of a helicopter—all of these visual and auditory cues fit into Nanu's understanding of where she is. In time, the smell of that machine will permeate her world and two-legged ones will spill out of it to harass her.

Now that she's ashore, however, another deadline looms. Barring a chance meal on a beached whale or maybe a caribou calf if she gets lucky, or a serving of eggs, birds, ground squirrels and plant material, her supply of energy will be finite. She must exert herself as little as possible. She can sleep in the shade of shrubbery when she is hot, and try not to burn energy to heat herself when the temperature drops. But she cannot feast on seal fat because the seals, her preferred prey, are long gone and out of reach, chasing shoals of fish wherever they may roam.

The world she now occupies, though in some respects as featureless and flat as the ice stretching west to the horizon, is a more static place than the one she experienced through the dark winter. Ice is in constant motion. Pressure ridges shift and change as the winter progresses. On ice, plains can become mountains almost overnight.

In contrast, land changes much more slowly. This shoreline around Churchill, where once a Hudson's Bay Company fur-trading post stood, has been rising at a rate of only a fraction of an inch per year since the weight of the last great ice sheets was released centuries ago, known in geological terms as isostatic rebound, or post-glacial rebound. Evidence of this can be found in the sinewy lines of sand and gravel on the beaches where once the tide cycled in and out. Some of these so-called beach ridges are now distant from today's shoreline. The farther these are from the current edge of the water, the better drained they will be. In time, habitation by birds, animals and hardy colonizing plant species will create nutritious "soil" above permafrost, for shrubby plants and even small trees, like tamarack and black spruce, to get a toehold. Each ridge—each food source habitat or denning opportunity afforded by these lines of nonfrozen, more fertile ground—is written somehow into Nanu's body and memory. However, in recent years, the slow yet inexorable rise of global sea levels through global warming confounds her. Where bears once might have been able to predict the gentle rising of the land from isostatic rebound, now those changes in elevation are offset to some small degree by rising waters of the ocean.

Nanu must know this place well to survive. To thrive. But unlike her life on the ice, which is constantly shifting, her life on land focuses on one specific goal: finding a safe place to build a den. While she could consider denning right at the coast—luckily, the concentration of other polar bears from the southwest Hudson Bay population is still very low—there are other bears who will be getting hungrier by the week, as they forage along the foreshore lands. A better plan is to expend energy on a slow walk inland over the hottest summer months in the hopes of finding a safe place. And so she rambles on, searching for the den she built the year before.

But now there are new threats, particularly the barren-land grizzly and even black bears. Wolves, too, or perhaps even wolverines might find their way to her secret place. Still, the drive to find a place to nest surpasses these risks. Leaving the water of the great bay behind, she dries in the sun as she walks. She puts one foot in front of the other, as she did on the ice, leaving a line of beautiful footprints in tidal mud and then in the sand. Were she eating more, in addition to the footprints there might be the occasional pile of scat to indicate her passing. When she transitions onto tussock tundra on higher ground, she is leaving almost no visible trace of her passing at all, except the odd clot of transparent white hair that she is shedding to cool her body and to refresh her sumptuous coat before she settles into a den to await the arrival of the next generation.

—

By August, she is nearly forty-five miles inland from the coast and ghosting through places that have a very familiar feel, for this is the territory where she was born eight years ago and within range of where she denned this time last year. Her nose is, as always, an asset in determining threats but also in creating a picture of who is here and who *was* here. Perhaps she even catches her own scent on the wind in familiar haunts from other years.

What is different this year, as she moves into the creek bed that has been her destination, is that fire has clawed its way through the ground brush. Where once there were essences of eggs and young birds, droppings, fox kits and other summer tundra dwellers, there is now only the sting of burned wood and rain-soaked soil. Although she has not yet experienced fire directly, she has smelled smoke on the wind this year, seen it in the air.

Today, though, it's not fire but rain that she must deal with. Another line squall moves through with a row of black clouds that looks like an ocean wave cresting. The sound and the fury of this summer storm, under shearing clouds in tumultuous skies, make her wince. The severe weather that has soaked her to the bone is a welcome relief from the heat. She isn't cold when the rain lashes down, or even noticeably wet at skin level. And out of such tumult comes a gift: a big male woodland caribou electrocuted by lightning. She hunkers down to see what little fat might be left after his burned frame has been scavenged by other creatures.

With some meat finally in her stomach, she carries on inland, following a large creek that eventually peters out in a modest cut through the tundra. Persisting in her search, stopping often to sniff the wind and orient herself in relation to the land, the sun, the wind and the night sky, Nanu eventually finds the familiar creek bed where spruce roots and a fallen tree have created a hollow. When she chose the place the previous year, she knew the prevailing northerly winds of winter would create a substantial snowdrift on top of roots and branches. Here, she had fashioned her first maternity den. Here, she will begin again.

While the soil is still supple and unfrozen, she digs around and creates a bit of a platform where she starts sleeping regularly as the days shorten and the temperatures drop. On mornings after nights when the temperature drops below freezing, water in the soil freezes and pushes up tiaras of filigreed ice that crush easily under her as she rolls. But as winter looms, the ground is less moist, and with a covering of grass and eventually snow, she knows that this is the foundation of a place she will easily be able to heat with her own body as deep cold settles in.

Once more, Nanu positions the door of her den away from the prevailing winds, and as new snow starts to fall, she piles and pats it around an opening, careful to direct any wind-driven snow away from the opening itself.

By October, when the edges of tundra ponds and sloughs are crazy-paved with new ice, Nanu is settled in her spot, sleeping and resting for most of the day to conserve energy. Eventually, when snow falls regularly and the winter winds blow, a drift forms along the edge of the stream bank that envelops her. With each subsequent layer of insulation and building material that blows in, she scratches and scrapes, pushes and shapes until she is totally enclosed in a cocoon of new snow, glazed on the inside by her breath and the radiated heat of her body.

The den into which the cubs will be born is far more than a hole in the snow. From the early days of formation, as new snow has fallen—even more remarkable when one considers her sleepy state—Nanu keeps an exit tunnel close to the surface of the downgrade snow. Bit by bit, she has lengthened the den on a regular basis by digging it out with her claws. Much like the anatomy of her own expanding womb, there is a smaller tunnel that leads toward the outside and, up inside, is a bigger space where she resides. Early on, extra snow will be pushed out the exit tunnel. But as time moves on, and her radiant heat is absorbed by the internal walls, the space expands ever so slightly, and she packs out a flat platform on which she can rest without sliding down the exit tunnel. The magic of this design lies in the creation of a space that, while close to freezing, still allows for body warmth to shape its walls. Through a little chimney she has scraped above, new air enters the den. Like the exit tunnel, this hole has to be tended as well, to ensure that it lets in sufficient fresh air without causing too much heat loss.

As this process of denning continues, as if by magic, one little ball of cells at a time in her uterus awakens. Fully five months after mating and conception, the growth of this year's brood continues. If all goes well, in only thirty more days, there will be three bears sharing this one sheltered place.

Outside, the sun moves to its southernmost position over the earth. The lands surrounding Nanu are winter dressed, like sugared icing. Moonshine and a gentle spatter of starlight dance blue shadows from here to there, and back again, as the sky turns. Arches of frozen red dogwood branches and alder catkins mask pure white Arctic hares and twitchy ptarmigan, nibbling away, waiting for spring. Quiet hearts beat in hidden places around the den, echoed only by the scurrying of lemmings on grass pathways below. Above, from time to time, Nanu hears the quiet footsteps of the fox on her daily prowl. Her tracks whisper to the snowy owl where a next meal might be.

Nanu has been in her den now for fully two moons. Any appearance of light from without has diminished with the falling away of the sun but also with the thickening of the snow cover. At one point, when the chimney was fully blocked with caked snow, she scratched her way out through the exit tunnel to make adjustments in the hole itself on the outside but also to make other adjustments inside the den as well. She scratches with a stone carver's precision to widen the chimney. How she knows to do this, whether she senses a decrease in the amount of fresh air available to her or whether there is some other motive, is part of the great mystery. Nothing at this point is more important than putting energy into the developing fetuses within her womb, except perhaps the maintenance of the womb of ice in which the entire drama is taking place.

She has been here before, waiting. The sensation of decreasing comfort with staying in one position—on one side, on the other, on her front, or on her back with legs reaching up into the space of the den—is familiar. Her time has nearly come. Her stomach has long since stopped growling. The sedges and grasses she consumed on windblown beach ridges before actually committing to enter the den serve as a bolus or placeholder, so that her stomach and digestive system will not contract completely from lack of use during this fasting time.

Even in her state of semi-suspended animation, somewhere between sleep and wakefulness, using as little energy as possible, Nanu stands. She moves. She stands. She sits. She lies on one side. She hefts herself over to the other. She turns onto her back, stretching her forelegs out until they touch one side of the den, then stretches her back legs out until they touch the other. She stands again and sniffs the vent to make sure there is sufficient outside air still filtering in. She moves down toward the exit, into what is effectively a second room in the den, and there does it all over again. Waiting. Just waiting, oblivious to a world without and beyond that is changing at rates and in ways she and her cubs may never comprehend.

Things progress until her pregnancy gets to the point where Nanu is moving more than she is resting in any one position. Her four nipples are starting to swell and leak. She arches over when sitting up and licks to clean herself. With the change of position, the rippling of the muscles in her abdomen gives way to disorganized pinching in her back end that gives way, in turn, to regular rolling contractions.

Finally, on the day the northern hemisphere reaches the center of its darkest night—the winter solstice—after more than twenty-four hours of muscular rhythms through her abdomen, she stands to change her position yet again and behind her, between her back legs in the darkness, silently drops a new life that takes its first breath with a nearly inaudible mew.

She reaches around and licks the newcomer—for the purposes of my story, drawing on the language of the Inuit, Inuktitut, we'll call her Sivulliq, the first one. Nanu coddles the newborn in her forepaws. Gently, with claws that are longer and three times the thickness of those new little down-covered legs, she nudges the tiny one up between her legs and onto her belly. In addition to the smell of her mother, which will become so reassuring, so familiar, Sivu experiences the rippling contractions that herald her brother's birth. Together, they welcome Kingulliq, the last one, who arrives just less than an hour later. In the nourishing confines of this remarkable enclosure, a bond is formed that—fate preserve it—will bind these three lives inextricably for two years or maybe more in perilous times.

four
Birthing

ᐋᒡᔪᓕᖅᖃᒃ ᑕᐅᖃᒡᔪᐊᖅᒃ ᑎᓯᐱᕆ

Appearing Moon

DECEMBER

What has happened here is nothing short of miraculous. Centuries of evolutionary adaptation have created a process whereby tiny, defenseless creatures can be born into one of the most forbidding environments on earth, and still thrive. A mother who has not eaten since leaving the ice, now nearly six months ago, is able to nourish her cubs in utero and yet still keep her metabolism quiet enough to conserve energy for at least three more months of fasting to come. Because, in addition to her own considerable insulation—two inches of thick downy underfur combined with a full mantle of long hollow guard hairs—every bear has her coating of fat just below the skin. The well-insulated snow cave that is the den can be warmed to just below freezing with nothing more than the presence of a warm bear.

To save energy, Nanu is able to lower her body temperature slightly from its normal 37°C. Any wastes from her bodily processes are reabsorbed, so that the den remains clean, with nothing to feed microbes or bacteria that could potentially harm her young. In her state of suspended animation in the darkened confines of the den, she delivers two blind, deaf, toothless, downy-haired young who are less than 1 percent of her size, with no body fat to speak of. The self-regulating birth process then starts the steady production of milk, nourishment with 32 percent fat that not only keeps these tiny helpless newcomers alive, but allows them to thrive, when the temperatures outside can be as far below zero as their mother's body temperature is above.

The floor plan of the den resembles that of a conventional Inuit iglu. The original lair—shaped by the digging that Nanu did in the stream bank before the ground froze, before the snow started falling—has been expanded. The upper room is now nearly two yards in diameter and half a yard higher than the exit tunnel. The genius of the design is that as air is warmed by Nanu's body and breath, it forms a bubble of warmth that rises into this upper space. This is the most comfortable part of the den. If cold air flows in through the vent or in the exit tunnel, it settles in the lower chamber where it cannot harm the new arrivals. The lower chamber is slightly narrower but still able to accommodate any movements Nanu may need to make.

Sivu and Kingu will not appreciate the brilliance of this ingenious structure initially, for the first world they inhabit after arrival is almost functionally the same as the home they have grown in since conception. Instead of being immersed in amniotic fluid, they are immersed in the warm air trapped in the fur of Nanu's belly, where the sound of their mother's slow-beating heart is as present and familiar as it was when they were in utero.

On arrival, the cubs are covered with a dusting of fine hair over pink skin. The only dark pigment visible is on their little noses and footpads, which gets blacker with time. In the first few weeks, as their mother's rich milk powers their exponential growth in size, the cubs' skin turns to gray, except around the eyes, lips and muzzle, which turn black by the time they are three weeks old.

As the cubs' skin darkens, their downy natal dress is replaced by the dense undercoat and longer guard hairs they will keep through to adulthood. By twenty-five days old, the soles of their little five-toed feet start developing hair as well, completing the insulation they need for moving, when the time is right, away from their mother and around the den, without undue heat loss.

The cubs' first full month of existence is without sight, which, in a way, is nature's practice for the hunting they will do in the long winter night, using every sense but sight. Before their eyes open early in the second month, they learn to navigate with other developing senses, often with Nanu's gentle guidance. They learn to feed and start to differentiate the textures, smells, vibrations, and rhythms in the den.

And so the gradual development of the cubs from total dependence to independence begins. Their ears open and their hearing starts by their second month of life. Their deciduous milk teeth—the ones that will be pushed out by their permanent dentition—come in as well. By two months of age, their musculoskeletal development and coordination are developing in earnest. First, similar to other mammalian babies, the head and neck are raised. Then they are able to prop themselves on their elbows, reach a doglike sitting position and finally raise themselves up on their hind legs in preparation for learning to walk, sometime in their third month of life, in the den.

Producing milk that is one third fat means that Nanu is losing weight almost as fast as the cubs are gaining it, at least two pounds per day. The cubs double in size monthly—going from two to four pounds in January, from four to nine in February. By March, when they are starting to actually explore the inside of the den, they have more than doubled in weight again and are in the twenty-four to twenty-six-pound range and increasingly aware of their surroundings. The cubs' digestive systems are so efficient that most of the nutrition they consume aids their growth.

But what is happening in this remarkable incubator tucked into the side of an unnamed creek forty-three miles inland from the coast of Hudson Bay, south of Churchill, Manitoba, is more than just growth. The constant proximity of the three bears is creating a family bond that will see them through to separation and independence that is at least two years off. Sounds, smells, touches, reactions, sensations of pleasure or pain—the three bears bond with one another as polar bears have done down the centuries. And all within a cocoon of warmth existing in one of the most challenging environments on earth.

Outside, the air is dry and supremely cold. White foxes, using their own strategies to keep warm and to conserve energy, roust small mammals, like lemmings, that eke out a living in the tundra grasslands under the snow. The presence of a fox outside the den may, in fact, be something that the cubs perceive by sound, or scent, or perhaps even by the energy the foxes add to the neighborhood.

Similarly, there will be ptarmigan and hares hiding in nooks behind ancient glacial erratics where the snow does not swirl, eating whatever they can find in the frozen catkins or dwarf birch or alder shrubs, perhaps making their presence known or felt to the residents of the den as well. And, as spring once again creeps north, there might be a snowy owl or two who, with the certainty of their gifts, score meals of unsuspecting furred or feathered prey. None of these creatures is doing anything other than surviving. Yet inside the den, the bear is raising her young through the darkest and coldest part of the winter—a testament to the art of survival.

—

One day, the piercing sound of a machine—a helicopter dropping grid stakes for a mining claim in the area—startles the cubs. The noise, even filtered through the den wall, is like nothing they have ever experienced. At first they continue their explorations around the den, but the noise gets louder and louder until they cluster back into Nanu's bosom, where all is warm and safe.

But by degrees, they get stronger and start exploring the den more confidently. First, Sivu, who is by far the more precocious of the two, rolls over the lip of the upper platform. Failing to get back up, she mews mightily until her mother rouses and scoops her back up to safety.

With time, Sivu is driven to explore even more. Her claws

get stronger. Her ability to move on all fours improves, and before long she is galloping over the edge. Kingu is always a bit more tentative. He eventually follows his sister, and as Nanu dozes, there is much scuffling at the other end of the den, before the two of them are back for milk.

By March, their third month of development, the cubs are getting their lower incisors and canine teeth. When they pinch Nanu during nursing, she reprimands them. In this final month in the den, it is clear that the cubs' hearing is starting to get much more acute. They can now hear the fox walking over the den. They startle more easily. And, as they pounce and roll together, they try out different voices and calls that become part of everyday chatter in the den. Each night they collapse into a heap and purr contentedly on or near their mother as they drift off to sleep.

With all this activity, Nanu must rouse herself from her sleepy state to tend the den, scraping the frost that builds up on the walls. By now, the last of her molted hairs are distributed over the floor and elsewhere. Hairs that have rubbed off onto the ceiling hang like stalactites in a cave. From time to time, she pokes at the air vent, ensuring there is still plenty of fresh air.

After the equinox on March 21, when the sun is visible for twelve hours, the days lengthen quickly. The moon cycles overhead, sprinkling moonbeams into the darkness of the den. For the first time, Nanu can see her cubs. She senses the moment has come.

After summer, fall and now winter, Nanu's old self is stirring inside her, and she is starting to think about readying the family to move. It is forty-three miles to the edge of the bay. The cubs are getting stronger every day, and soon it will be time to introduce them to the light outside and to get the three of them on their way.

There is nothing but uncertainty ahead, as there has been for every emerging mother bear since the beginning. But now, who knows? How strong are they? How vulnerable are they? Will they be able to deal with the threats ahead?

By March's end, Nanu is fully awake and attending to her world, playing with the cubs when they are awake, too, sleeping with them when they are tired. As a new moon heralds April, the nights get shorter. Light creeps in through the air vent above. The cubs are more active than ever, fearless little fur balls with claws and teeth. Nanu knows the sounds, the patterns. Nanu knows when Sivu bites Kingu's nose until he cries. She watches as they chase each other from the upper chamber to the lower chamber and back again. When a piece of ice breaks off the roof, they start using it as a ball. Propelled by a little white paw, the ice ball flies through the air immediately underneath the air vent. A tiny ray of sunlight that has bounced down the vent momentarily illuminates the crystal, like a star in a changing universe.

The bears are ready to enter the wider world, a world where tradition and progress collide. Until very recently, the speed of change was gradual, so bears could mostly adapt as they went about their yearly cycles. Today, climate change has accelerated in lockstep with technological progress, and that change now takes place much more rapidly. Nanu and her cubs are living in circumstances that at almost every turn of fate will challenge their very survival.

five
Venturing

ᑎᓕᑉᔪᐃᑦ

Bearded Seal Pups Moon

APRIL

—

Though we can never know exactly what combination of factors triggers Nanu's move toward the exit tunnel with her cubs, about three months into their new lives she decides they have developed sufficiently to set and maintain their own temperatures without mother's help. By April, the outside temperatures have eased, and the cubs themselves, although still without any body fat to speak of, have come to a point when they are generating their own heat with their activity.

Every day since December, Nanu has converted more than two pounds of her own stored energy into milk that has doubled and redoubled the size of the cubs. The adult bear who eventually punches through to the sunshine of an April day on the barrens of the Hudson Bay lowlands, is a scant 550 pounds, something of a shadow of her ample pregnant self who settled in six months earlier. The sooner she is hunting again, the better.

The cubs have undergone equally dramatic growth—going from 1/500th of their mother's weight when they were born to 1/20th of her current weight. Their first blast of direct sunlight on crystalline spring drifts leaves them squinting as they tumble from the den. The texture of new, or relatively new, snow is something they have never experienced. While Nanu rests with just her shoulders hanging out of the exit, they bleat and squeal, perhaps from the surprise of rolling down the grade outside the entrance.

Beyond the safety of the den, the first thing Nanu does, as the cubs check back for reassurance, is sniff the air and scan slowly in all directions. After months of low light, it takes a while for her eyes to adjust to the sun as well, but what she commands visually from her perch at the opening of the den is a mere fraction of the geographic scope of information that comes to her on the wind. Vapors that might include odors of steel mills in the Ohio valley, faraway forest-fire smoke or notes of whatever is burning that day at the Churchill dump.

Stiffly, she drags herself completely out of the den, shakes vigorously and stands fully upright for the first time in six months. After a few more stretches, she heads up over the den to the edge of the creek bed, chuffing for the cubs to follow. Working her way to a gravelly ridge a few dozen yards uphill from the creek, she stands looking first one way and then another. Scanning the distance. Sniffing the air. For now, without the protection of the den, she knows instinctively how vulnerable she and the cubs are, how much energy and effort have been expended to get to this point in their cycle and how quickly that could all change.

It is a totally new world for the cubs. They rush to their mother for security as she drops back down on all fours, sits down and then rolls back against the hill, letting the cubs get close to nurse. As they are leaving the den for the first time, and suckling hungrily in the full light of day, the fat content of Nanu's milk is now at its absolute maximum and it will stay this way until they get to the ice. But the moment the cubs start into solid food, as they will when Nanu catches her first seal, the fat content of her milk will start declining. It will drop to between 27 to 28 percent by autumn, and continue getting less rich (and requiring less energy to produce) with each passing month, to less than 20 percent after a year. Nursing will slow and eventually stop before the cubs separate, after two years with their mother.

That first foray out of the den lasts no more than half an hour before Nanu leads the cubs back to the place they know mostly by smell and by feel. With the door to the outside world now open, she sleeps again while the cubs tumble about, fighting, climbing over her and finally rolling into the warmth and protection of her forepaws. In no time, the three of them are asleep.

Over the next week, Nanu and the cubs venture farther and farther from the den, working their way increasingly up the ridge. Each time Nanu heads up the ridge, she stops at a place where the wind has scoured the ground, keeping it relatively snow-free with a variety of alpine grasses exposed. As she did on her way to build the den, she grazes on these freeze-dried grasses to reduce her hunger and to reawaken her digestive system with roughage.

Nanu has an extraordinary digestive system. On the ice, she can eat dozens of pounds of fat and protein when she is hunting seal. During the winter months, she can put her digestive tract into hibernation. In spring, before she heads back to the bay, she grazes on tundra grasses to keep her stomach distended until such time as regular food is available. Although she lacks cellulase, the enzyme cows and caribou produce to digest plant material, she knows she must eat just enough to kick-start a system that has been effectively dormant since July.

Forays away from the den in these early days build and tone the cubs' muscles for the journey to the ice that is about to begin. But these walks are also about readying her own body for the long walk back to the bay. Like NASA astronauts who spend protracted time in space and must compensate for physical inactivity, Nanu ensures that her bones do not degrade in any way during the denning time. Her muscles need toning and building now.

—

The following day, a new fall of deep wet snow makes it impossible for the cubs to move at all. The night freeze hardens the slush and creates a hard shiny crust that leaves them, the next time out, scrabbling to stop from sliding on any downgrade.

A second freak rain, complete with April thunder and lightning, catches them farther away from the safety of the den than they should have been. Even with Nanu urging them to follow her as fast as they can, Sivu and Kingu are soaked. By the time they make it back to the den, they are both shivering uncontrollably. Although they are getting stronger and more coordinated with each foray into the outside world, the downpour reminds them of just how vulnerable they are against cold. Their fur is getting thicker by the day but they still have almost no fat beneath the skin to serve as insulation.

That night, the wind shifts back to the northwest, heralding a sunrise wash of warmer hues. Nanu decides it is time to move. In the ten days since she opened the den, the sea has been there on the wind. Silhouetted against the strengthening sun, the three bears walk away from the only place the cubs have known. Nanu is in the lead, the cubs roaming between her feet, getting sidetracked with smells and other distractions, catching up, getting ahead, being called back. They are always on the move, walking or climbing on their mother. Eventually, they lag enough for Nanu to stop, nurse and let them snuggle in for a snooze.

The route they are taking is similar to the one that Nanu first walked with her mother almost eight years ago to the day, and almost identical to the route she walked two years ago when hunger and the absence of live cubs had driven her from the den back to the ice. It isn't long before they are crossing a pattern of beach ridges, each one a little lower in elevation than the previous one.

They continue to nurse and rest. The cubs play less now because when they are not walking or nursing, they are sleeping. Their little feet, with their sensitive pores, learn with each step. Developing lungs inhale new ground with every breath, building body awareness of place. They feel the radiance of the sun as it moves from in front to beside and then behind them as the days progress. For Sivu and Kingu, this is all new, but for Nanu, they are familiar sensations from part of her memory, like melodies of a long-remembered tune.

Kingu, if he is to survive, will likely never come back this far inland, though he will know the essence of where he has come from for all of his days. As a male, he will den during the harshest months of winter, and he will bide his time on the shore during the summer fast. Sivu, by contrast, if she is to survive to reproductive maturity, become pregnant and come ashore seeking a safe den of her own one day—she will come here by heart, by the look and feel of the place—the sweet essence of ground-hugging spruce on the beach ridges, the faint smell of diesel from the trains running up and down the Hudson Bay Railway from Le Pas to Churchill, the pungent dens of foxes abandoned at this time of year, the feel of the wind, the warmth of the sun, the sounds of birds, only all in reverse order, retracing the line they are etching in the snow. Every step, every sight, every sound connects them to the vast beating Hudson Bay heartscape that is their home.

—

Suddenly Nanu stops with every muscle in her body flexed and ready. As if jerked back with an invisible hand on collar and lead, the cubs, too, tumble to a stop. Nanu sniffs and utters a high-pitched grunting sound that the cubs have never heard before—at least not at that intensity. Instead of suckling them or lying down to offer them respite from the cool winds and incoming weather, Nanu stands and sniffs, first in one direction, then in another and another, finishing with a long stand facing downwind.

It is only then that she sees the threat in the distance. Three gray wolves, not yet in any kind of formation, are making their way upwind. Had she not had such olfaction, picking up vapors that linger on the breeze, she would never have lived this long. Now she watches intently as these hungry animals circle downwind, hoping for a surprise attack.

Encouraging the cubs to keep close, she stands again resolutely so that the wolves can see her before taking a few vigorous running steps in their direction. She then continues walking toward the wolves, cubs behind her. Together, moving over the remains of drifts in the hollows and along the exposed lichen-encrusted gravel of the open beach ridges, they move on a line that will intersect with the wolves' line of travel. Even if the wolves are only adolescents, there are likely more mature ones in the vicinity. Undaunted, driven by a mother's combination of fear, caution and courage, Nanu chooses to pose a threat of her own.

Again, she stands, radiating the confidence of size. This time the wolves stop, look and then look away. Suddenly they turn and lope off in the other direction. For now, at least, the threat is gone. But the encounter is a reminder of just how vulnerable Nanu is with precious cargo in tow.

At this point in their lives, the cubs have no real capacity to run. Nanu will never leave them, except to fight on their behalf, so her ability to run in effect is compromised as well. Given their young age and lack of experience, the best she can do to protect the cubs is to encourage them to listen and to stay by. Which is exactly what they do as Nanu keeps following her nose toward salt water, increasing with every step the distance between the three bears and the three wandering young wolves but decreasing the distance between where they are and threats that lie ahead.

Day six, in spitting gray snow, they crest a ridge, and for the first time, the cubs, riding on their mother's back, sniff the air with their little black noses and sense that something is different. When their mother stands and sniffs the air, they tumble to the ground and get up on their little hind legs to do the same. A week of unlimited nutrition and exercise seems to have strengthened them and made them bigger, although, truth be told, when they stand on their hind legs beside their mother, they barely come up to her hip. From behind, Sivu on one flank, Kingu on the other, they are a tableau of strength and vulnerability.

But there is definitely something new in the air. For nearly a week, the world before them has looked flat and almost uniformly white. Now this world is shifting. For the first time, Sivu and Kingu are sensing, with their noses and in their mother's changed body language, the ice of Hudson Bay and the odor of muddy ice on the foreshore flats, the smell of their new home. Mixed with the familiar scents are old oil, which may have washed in from a summer boat at sea, and acrid plastic flotsam, which may have come from anywhere, increasingly brought to this place by the slow rotations of the Hudson Bay gyre.

At the beach, Nanu quickens her pace, then breaks into a short canter. Stopping suddenly, she flops onto her back and rolls for the longest time with her feet in the air and the cubs clambering all over her. She gets up, shakes and sniffs along a crack in the ice until she comes to a place where the tide has broken open a space down to the flats. She disappears momentarily down through the crack and reappears with a great tawny snake of bull kelp that she drags up on the ice. This is a much more substantial plant than anything she has found inland. It's full of alginates and fiber that will fill her digestive system and ready it for the meal that, with any luck at all, will be forthcoming in the hours or days to come. The little ones have a bit of a chew but tire of it quickly and butt their way in for milk instead.

In a familiar family line, they continue out onto the ice. The cubs are close because they sense their mother's change in body language, her higher level of general awareness. She stops and sniffs and stands much more often than she did while they were on the land. She and her cubs are entering a dangerous world of adult bears: females without cubs, who would probably ignore them, and males, ready to mate, whose first gambit would be to kill and eat the offspring of a competitor.

To be sure, male bears, young and old, have been out on the ice all winter, but with the lengthening of the days and the turning of their internal cycles, they are feeding and following the scent tracks of females. Now that Nanu, Sivu and Kingu are on the ice, the threat from these males is extreme. Attacks on new cubs and lactating females at this time of year are common. And if the males aren't attacking a trio like this for nutrition in a lean year, then they are attacking the cubs to kill them, in the hope that this might bring the female back into estrous. Either way, as hungry as Nanu is at this moment of return to the ice, she has to be ever vigilant to ensure that all the energy she has put into bringing cubs this far will not be lost in an attack by one of her own.

With the cubs tagging along, Nanu works every scent on the breeze, assessing the ice for signs of seal habitation. There are smells everywhere—of adult seals, young seals, seals that have been killed by other bears—the smells of other bears, the smells of foxes, the sights and sounds of returning birds. The olfactory range is far more intriguing than the endless ice.

The near-human voice of a raven and the piercing squawks of a glaucous gull draw Nanu's attention to a place far along a pressure ridge. Calling Sivu and Kingu to her side, she moves cautiously to the spot where the birds are calling and finds the remains of a ringed seal whitecoat probably killed several days before. It is mostly just furry skin left behind, but in spite of the protestations of the raven and the gull, she eats that and keeps moving along the crack. Suddenly she stops. She is sure she has located an aglu.

—

Hunting is a delicate business at the best of times. It requires stealth, discipline, patience and, most important, persistence. At this time of year, with the entire surface of the bay covered with ice, stationary hunting is the only and, happily, the preferred option in terms of success. But it works best when a bear is alone. Sivu and Kingu don't seem to understand at first why Nanu nudges them away. But in time, making as little noise and movement as possible, she brings them to a point a few yards from the aglu and does her best with gestures, low chuffing sounds and gentle encouragement to get them to lie still while she moves back to prepare for the kill.

She can hear that there is a young seal inside. With precision and care that seems to belie the size and strength of her paws, she scrapes away some of the snow covering the thin layer of ice that the heat of the birthing and activity of the seal would have created on the inside of her lair.

Sivu is keen to know what is going on. She is soon back beside her mother. Kingu is going to sleep, so he is no longer a potential problem here. Nanu pushes Sivu to her side and then, in a sitting position with her feet almost on what would be the apex of the dome of the aglu, she stiffens. Sivu takes one look at this and settles down quietly as well.

Nanu can hear the quiet mewing of the baby and its movements inside the lair. But that is not the meal she is hoping for. Eventually, she feels the puff of condensed air come up through the air hole in the aglu, followed by the hollow swoosh of water below. Finally, the slip of a wet mother seal crawling up out of the water into her lair to nurse.

In one smooth movement, forelegs braced, Nanu rises up and crashes down through the top of the aglu, front feet followed by her head. Then, to Sivu's amazement, she recoils back above the surface of the ice with a bloody seal four times the cub's size.

No time for lessons here. Nanu keeps her grip on the seal's fragile head with her teeth, her forepaw on the body until it stops moving. For the first time in nine months, starting at the seal's belly, she rips through the gray-silver fur and into the rich blubber that she has been craving. As the cubs approach, Nanu's face is covered with offal, but if bears could smile, she would be smiling through her bloodstained teeth. Actual seal fat is new to the cubs, as they have suckled on milk made of this comestible, but the taste is familiar. In no time, they are dabbling inside the carcass as well, and before long, they are colored red, too. Life on the ice has begun in earnest.

six
Learning

ᐃᕐᓂᐅᕐᓂᕐ

Pregnant Caribou Moon

MAY

—

Arriving at the ice midseason is new for Nanu. As a single bear, she would normally have been far out on the bay at this point with a good sense of where the seals were, where they were whelping, and where the hunting was best. This time, with Sivu and Kingu in tow, her challenge is to continue the process of instruction while finding a steady supply of food so that she can regain her strength and her weight for the uncertainties that lie ahead.

Thankfully, the cubs seem to sense that adapting to the ice is essential—for food, for renewal, for survival. Still, they tire on the journey; they lie down without provocation and fall behind. Sometimes, Nanu slows down and goads them with distance to catch up, with the promise of nourishment. Other times she cycles back, bumps them with her nose and makes "follow me" sounds.

This slower pace allows Nanu to expend less energy. The calories she is passing on through her milk are still the biggest drain on her resources, but she must also avoid getting overheated. With luck, they can locate good hunting places close to shore. If not, the movement out onto the ice will have to continue, but at a pace set by the little ones.

Near a rocky offshore island, they come to a place where currents, the heat of the sun on the dark rock, and pushes of wind and weather have created a place of broken ice that is moving back and forth with the tide. There will be other seals and probably pups in the vicinity of this open water, potentially other bears, too. The shallows around islands like this are invariably places where bird guano nourishes algae growth, which in turn feeds zooplankters and small fish that are the prey of bigger fish. Islands with surrounding open water are excellent places for seals to be and, of course, for hungry polar bears to hunt. Sure enough, in the middle of this zone, Nanu spies a couple of big ringed seals basking in the sunshine.

The cubs have no idea why Nanu is stopping and gauging the wind the way she is, but by now they have learned that when this happens, they should mimic their mother and stay quiet. In time, they will actually see or smell or hear what has caught her attention, but for now, all she expects them to do is mimic what she is doing. If they do not, she calls them to come close and to be quiet beside her. Kingu is usually the compliant one. Sivu, on the other hand, has a mind of her own.

Although the wind today is nothing more than a breeze from the west, it has to be assessed when planning a hunt.

With careful steps, Nanu circles around to the right, staying low on the ice and moving slowly toward a lead. The cubs follow.

From this new vantage point, it is easy to see that the closer of these two seals is sleeping on his side with his head tipped back, his nose almost touching the ice. When Nanu has circled to the point of being directly downwind, the place where the seal has the least chance of catching her scent, the cubs finally start to grasp what stealth maneuvering is all about. They, too, stop in their little tracks and start sniffing the air with gusto. No doubt, they are smelling something different, something that they may well be remembering through their genes. Perhaps it is the familiar, faintly fishy smell of their mother's milk.

Nanu glides to a small pressure ridge in the ice, out of direct sight of the seals, and lies down to nurse. When the cubs have had their fill, they bundle in beside her, one on top of the other, and nod off to sleep. Effortlessly, Nanu slips into the lead. She surfaces silently like a slow-moving ice floe and begins closing the distance between herself and the sleeping prey.

When Nanu is within one hundred yards of the seal, he lifts his head. Nanu stops. All that shows in the water is white forehead with black eyes and nose, and a line of dry fur along her back, all of which could easily be patterns in the ice itself. After a minute or so, the seal's big eyes get heavy. Eventually, they close and his head rolls back to where it was before.

Nanu starts to move again, almost imperceptibly in the water.

On these stealth hunts, Nanu has learned to fix the position of the prey on whatever ice pan it is using for a basking place and to note where the shortest distance to the water is. And then she starts moving toward that position. From the seal's point of view, all is well. But from moment to moment, the bear is in a different place, and always closer.

While this hunt progresses, Sivu awakens and becomes curious to know where her mother is. She starts calling. This wakes her brother. Just as Nanu takes a deep breath and submerges for the swim that should end in a meal, the cubs begin calling and trotting up the side of the lead in the direction of the seal, who awakes with a start and, without delay, dives off the far side of the ice pan and into the open water.

Nanu explodes from the water only to land on an empty place where the seal had been. Undaunted and still in hot pursuit, she takes three powerful steps across the rocking ice pan and dives off the other side, hoping to catch the seal perhaps curling back out of surprise or indecision. But it is long gone. Their meal will have to wait for another day.

—

Springtime auroras swirling gossamer tulles of delicate rose and aquamarines in the last of winter's darkness give way to sunshine from 4:00 a.m. to 10:00 p.m. By then, cubs have had many lessons in stationary hunting. They have learned where to look for food and how best to spend their time. They have learned that different seals have different tolerances for disturbance. Like birds and bears, for that matter, some are skittish and some are more placid, but not for long. Following Nanu's lead, they learn about moving downwind, about advancing on a seal. They learn about patience. They learn about hunger.

And they learn about the rewards of taking one's time with the hunt.

They also learn about the Indigenous people with whom they have shared the ice for thousands of years. Generations ago, this scenario would be played out with the canid prints, the smell of dogs and two-legs, and the thin parallel lines of iced qamutiik, or sled, runners cutting through the wind ridges on the snowed surface of the ocean. Today, however, between the runners are the corrugated tracks of snow machines that smell more of smoke and two-legs than anything the polar bears are familiar with. Ever curious, Sivu and Kingu fall into line behind their mother, who adds her prints to the linear snow pastiche moving toward the floe edge. Her hind feet step exactly into the prints of her forefeet, leaving the distinct impression, except for the occasional claw marks, that a two-leg is walking with two gamboling bear cubs as part of the hunting procession.

By and by, they come to a place near the floe edge where many tracks intersect and the snow and ice are marked with blots of seal blood and a welter of other scents; some familiar, some not. There is a curved windbreak wall of blocks cut from the packed surface of snow, discarded tent pegs and a nearly overwhelming smell of two-legs. With them are bones and well-carved remains of a couple of big seals, perhaps shot while basking in the spring sun. Had Nanu moved into the area a day or two earlier, this scene might have been very different.

Nanu picks at the carcasses and licks the blood-soaked snow, but knowing that the nutrition that might be gleaned from an old Inuit hunting camp is not what they need to build body stores for the pending summer fast, she urges the cubs to move along. Out along the floe edge they go, their own little parade of three, to where the chance of similar late-season hunting success will be higher without the leavings of this earlier two-legged hunt.

—

By June, as meltwater pools transform the surface of the ice into a sun-warmed blotter of azure blue on white, the young ones have tasted mature seal blubber several more times. Because they have just caught the tail end of the seal-pupping season, they have also had an opportunity to feed on young seals. Nanu's successful hunt of a small adult seal ends with a feed of meat and, as important for the cubs, a tug-of-war over a discarded little seal flipper.

As the ice rots under the relentless late-spring sun, the cubs have doubled again in size. Sivu is now nearly forty-four pounds. When he is fully grown, Kingu will almost certainly end up being twice the size of his sister. He is already starting to look noticeably bigger, thicker through the chest, higher in the shoulder, more round in the rump. When they stand together he is somewhere between his sister's and his mother's heights. But it is Kingu who is behind Sivu when it comes to anything new or potentially alarming. She is his protector.

Nanu's internal clock ticks on. She must find sufficient success in her hunting to ensure that she has enough stored energy to see the cubs all through another summer fast. And, as has been happening in recent years, the sun seems hotter and the ice seems to be decaying earlier than she remembers in her genes. The drip, drip, drip of melting pressure ridges might as well be the tick, tick, tick of accelerated time in a fast-changing world.

The listening comprehension of the cubs is developing almost as fast as their bodies. Their repertoires of responses are increasing as well. They have both learned and practiced an everyday vocabulary of vocalizations, whether it is communicating between themselves—cub talk—or communicating with their mother. And although Nanu has done her best to keep them out of the water, because of their susceptibility to cold, they have also learned from their various immersions— accidental and intentional—that the underwater environment is full of pressure waves and sounds that are essential cues in their world as well. They watch their mother take exploratory dives under the ice or along the ice edge. Just as the sounds on the surface of the ice offer clues about who is near, so the water transmits vibrations effectively as well. There is so much to learn.

Today, Nanu spies another biggish bearded seal basking on the edge of the floe against a long lead. She makes another stealth approach by water, having left the cubs to sit quietly. They are encamped within sight, well downwind, and sufficiently far away so as not to pose any kind of threat to the seal, but they are cubs, and with them, she has learned, nothing is predictable. All they can do, all they have learned to do, all they must do to ensure their next solid meal, is watch as their mother drifts toward the unsuspecting seal like a surfacing submarine rigged for silent running.

The seal has two escape options. The obvious one is the open lead in front of its position on the floe. But on her reconnaissance of the situation, Nanu has determined that behind the seal, as evidenced on the ice by birthing marks and lines of blood and feces across the surface toward a dark spot on the ice, there is a "back" exit to this basking location in the form of a well-worn breathing hole.

As the cubs watch, she continues—slowly, steadily. But today, instead of planning for the frontal approach over the edge of the floe, she is physically coiling in the water for something quite different. When the seal raises its head to sniff the breeze, Nanu lies completely still in the water. The season's bounty—four to six inches of blubber over her whole body—makes her float higher in the water than she did in April.

Within pouncing range, Nanu breaks the surface with her forepaws and pulls her head up so that the seal flees toward the aglu. But instead of powering out of the water, Nanu arches her back and dives down under the ice. With two sweeping strokes and rapid kicks to add to the force of the locomotion, she zooms along the undersurface of the ice and into the aglu from below. Just as the seal is diving down through the breathing hole, her powerful jaws grab and crush its head from below.

Nanu surfaces triumphantly with the bloody seal in her jaw. She hefts the seal, about half her weight, and herself out of the water and onto the ice. After she and the cubs eat, they sleep beside the kill. The fox feasts again quietly, then slips away. With no other bears around, Nanu takes a few days with this kill. But she senses the sun getting hot and high and, with those subtle changes, senses that the end of hunting for this season is not far off.

The wind changes suddenly. The temperature plummets. The water on the surface of the ice and in the leads around them crystallizes to clear black ice. The uncharacteristic near-summer temperatures earlier this spring have allowed the air to absorb much more moisture than usual. Now a hard cold in June creates crystals that begin as minor imperfections in the surface of the new ice, and then rise into the air for an inch or so. Surrounded by a forest of giant ice crystals, the three of them lie in a frozen world as the Arctic sun filters through the crystals onto the ice around them. Nanu has experienced nothing like this before.

With the change in pressure and temperature, another front roars in on a freshening southwesterly wind that brings with it an uncharacteristic flurry of heavy spring snow. The bears let the drifts settle and build around them. Shifting where they lie, they expand the den space. For nearly seventy hours, they are unable to move as the ice floe snaps, shudders and moves with the force of currents below and swirling winds above.

This freak spring storm has completely changed their world. For four days, they have ridden a floe powered by the unrelenting wind and current. Now the leads are open again, but the stars, when the night sky finally clears, are different. And the weight of the snow has pushed down the ice, and water has seeped onto the surface and created slush almost everywhere they might want to walk. Through the combined forces of wind, current and temperature, they have moved farther east in Hudson Bay than Nanu has ever been.

Nanu's mother had known a spring world of vast sky and ice with occasional leads of open water. Now Nanu lives in a world with wet skies, more water and altogether less ice. One day, they are walking on ice. The next, the weather changes abruptly—bringing more open water with sporadic floes of disintegrating ice. After this freak storm, the bears find themselves floating on a melting piece of ice in open ocean. The positioning of the stars, the smell of the air, the feel of the place—everything has changed.

Like the two-legs who have been roaming the circumpolar world for about the same length of time, polar bears know well how to navigate by the sun and by the stars. They have been doing so, in one form or another, for two hundred thousand years or more. The best ice Nanu can see from her raft is to the north and east. To the west and south, directions she would typically walk on solid ice at this time of year, there is only water. No land in sight.

Adding to the confusing smell of rotting ice and sea are vapors of oil that she has never experienced, at least not this clearly, and not at this time of year. They can stay on the floe and circle north and east, but instinct tells Nanu that this is not what she should be doing. Their only option is to head in the direction she knows and swim for shore, which is somewhere beyond the horizon. Ten miles, twenty? Maybe farther.

—

The young ones have grown. Sivu is 88 pounds and Kingu is nearly 110 pounds and to their muscle and bone tissue has been added a small amount of fat. Their coats are thick and full, and that is a good thing. Underfur, almost as dense as their mother's, will trap water against their skin and allow it to warm and remain there like a diver's wet suit. The colder water that passes by as they swim will slide over the longer guard hairs. And the exertion of their young muscles will produce heat, as long as they have food resources available to make those muscles work. Grown or not, they must swim or drown.

Nanu cannot force them to nurse but does her best, allowing them all the time they can to eat. Sivu seems to understand and fills herself to capacity, but Kingu seems more interested in worrying a gull that is picking at the remains of their last seal. Twilight falls and the sky clears. The air is warm. To the gentle chiming of jostling candle ice, Nanu slips into the water and circles back to encourage the cubs to follow. In no time, the floe edge is far behind. The darkness that lies ahead contains only water. Regulating her speed, Nanu stays just far enough ahead of the cubs to keep them motivated.

After three hours in the water, they have slowed and the cubs are starting to call when she gets too far ahead. Kingu, who seems to be in a world of his own, is swimming parallel to his mother on a path that is diverging to the south. But he seems strong and is keeping up. Sivu is falling behind, grasping Nanu's rump with her little forepaws to try to hitch a ride. She is hungry and exhausted. It's not the icy water that tires her. Her new coat provides some body heat as does her exertion. It is the absence of her mother's energy-loaded milk.

This is the longest she and Kingu have gone without nursing in their lives. If only they could rest. Three hours in the water turn into four, then five and six. Nanu looks to her left to see where Kingu is and spots a strange rainbow-coloured reflection of the night sky on the water around him.

Kingu is tiring and heading for his mother. His face is still white but his back is now streaked black, and he is leaving threads of oil in the water as he makes his way toward them.

He, too, is cold and getting colder. The sight, the smell, the sound of her approaching cub is unlike anything Nanu has seen. By the time she is able to sniff land, she has two sodden cubs taking turns clinging to her back for even a moment of warmth.

After eleven hours of swimming, Nanu's feet touch the tidal mud in several feet of water. The last obstacle is not the walk to shore, however—it is a wall of landfast ice that has remained on shore while the rest of the ice was blown out to sea. The cubs have survived more than twenty-five miles of open sea, but they lack the energy to clamber up to safety.

Nanu grabs them one at a time and struggles to set them up on the ice barrier. Kingu is now covered with oil and shivering. Sivu is shivering, too. Nanu does her best to bring them close so that they can benefit from her warmth and nurse, but neither has energy to eat. They fall asleep in their mother's embrace on the ice. Nanu frantically licks at Kingu to try to clean the oil from his fur. In time, they wake, slightly warmer, slightly rested. In a safe place now, they can repair themselves.

—

On the southwestern shores of Hudson Bay, the bears' journey has taken them, perhaps, to a safer place, but Kingu has swum through a surface slick of diesel fuel or heavy oil. Although Fort Severn and Peawanuck, the two Cree communities nearest the spot where the bears encountered the spill, are supplied by sea most often from Moosonee, because of the counterclockwise currents, it is much more likely that oil would have originated somewhere up the west coast of Hudson Bay, in the process of supplying Inuit communities like Arviat, Tikirarjuaq, Kangiq-liniq, Igluligaarjuk, Qamanittuaq or Salliq, and moved south and east with the water and the ice through the winter season.

In spite of strict rules for oceangoing vessels to prove their seaworthiness and stringent environmental regulations to ensure the safe movement of hydrocarbons by land, sea and air, spills still happen. With changing tides and increasing amounts of sediment being carried by northern rivers—slowed through the installation of hydro dams—ships, tugs and barges have increasing difficulty getting close to northern communities, many of which are located at the mouths of freshwater rivers, to unload their cargo. Hoses break, connections fail and the operators themselves, trying to do business in often marginal circumstances, may delay maintenance or reduce staff to improve the short-term profitability of their businesses. And it doesn't take much oil to make an environmentally significant spill.

Most fuel is lighter than water but heavier than ice. When on the surface, as much as 40 percent of diesel, for example, will evaporate, even in the cold, leaving heavier distillates behind. These can be broken up and dispersed by the energy of a storm on open ocean, or pool under ice when it forms, or be integrated into the brine channels, pores, air bubbles and other complexities of the ice itself. Whatever the fuel, it can be devastating to the feathers, skin or coat of a seabird or mammal.

Diesel fuel powers almost everything in northern communities nowadays—a dependence that brings with it significant environmental risks. But the traditional lamp, the qulliq, though perhaps seemingly now largely redundant or symbolic to southern sensibilities, is as important as it ever was in pre-contact times because it is the glow of this ancient lamp that illuminates and warms the collective soul of bear people around the circumpolar world. Similarly, the traditions of family and community—linked to the realities and rhythms of nature through the capture of seals, bears, birds, fish and whales—are perhaps even more essential than they were before Europeans sailed north into the land they called Ultima Thule, because in the circularity of life and death and life and death again, the seals, bears, birds, fish, whales and people are as one. So while the coating of one young bear in oil may seem small in the overall scheme of Arctic affairs, it is a problem that stretches to the very core of humanity's most intractable threat—ourselves.

seven

Tagged

ᓴᔅᒥᓇᕐᕕᒃ ᓴᔅᒐᐴᑦ ᔪᓚᐃ

Thin Hair Moon II

JULY

After more than twenty-four hours of nothing but sleep interspersed with nursing, Nanu is able to encourage the cubs to move inland to a mossy hollow in a copse of spruce. It is more of a forest than she has ever encountered in her life, a new and unfamiliar place.

She turns to Kingu, who sleeps soundly with his sister against his belly, and continues the process of cleaning the black off his fur. They are all to some degree streaked and stained with the fuel. But Kingu is the one who actually swam through the slick. Cold, hungry and exhausted, he is in no shape to tend to his personal hygiene. So she gently massages the compromised cub with her tongue, swallowing the petroleum as it is lifted from his fur. She rakes his coat with her claws, as much to rouse the cub as to clean him, still not sure what they had encountered in the water.

One of Kingu's eyes is partially closed and inflamed by the sticky material, his breathing seems labored, and his appetite is nothing like his sister's. It has taken him an eternity to get warm, longer than his sister, even though he is in direct contact with the radiance of his mother's skin.

During the next two days, they stay close to the sheltered nook in the trees. Slowly the cubs recover. Kingu shivers unusually, particularly at night, because the oil has destroyed the loft in his fur. Between nursings and snoozes in the sun, they take turns bathing themselves and one another. Nanu has shown, by example, that this location, a soft bed of sphagnum moss on the ground, covered with layers of spruce needles, is an ideal place to roll and scratch on back and sides.

Nanu concentrates on one side, pushing herself along the ground with all four feet paddling and scraping the ground to move herself forward. And then she rolls and twitches with her legs in the air. Tipping over onto the other side, she starts the process all over again. Molting is starting, another good way to shed oiled fur. So each time she scratches, there are clots of white hair left on the ground, hair that in some instances is covered with raw oil.

If Sivu and Kingu have learned anything in their first seven months of life, it is to watch their mother and to copy what she does. Eventually, by following her example, their strength and energy returns. Kingu's night shivering slows and eventually stops. And the more they nurse, the more they move again, the more they restore their health. Had they been able to stay on the ice longer, they would have been fatter, particularly

Nanu. Kingu's appetite comes back and he nurses again with abandon. Slowly, his confidence and curiosity return as well. With his sister, he again starts to stray from their temporary nest among the trees.

As their young systems absorb the various toxins in the oil they have been exposed to, Nanu reads the place as she always does. The landscape is familiar, yet different. Sounds and smells of water and nesting shorebirds surround them, but among these trees are fewer ground-nesting gulls and geese. There are smaller birds in the grasses and in the woods. The land is similar to what she grew up in but not the same. It has more rolling ground and thicker vegetation.

And there are pervasive vapors of diesel, woodsmoke, burning garbage and people on the north wind. Normally, on coming ashore from the ice, Nanu would expect these to be faint, faraway, or closer but borne by a west or a south wind.

Traditionally on Hudson Bay, bears take their families north, getting to land, and work their way along the coast to where they will eventually meet winter creeping south from the pole as the length of days diminishes and the sun eventually disappears altogether. Nanu follows the tradition of turning north, taking extra care this time because of her general sense of disorientation. She knows that these smells bring with them potential new threats.

And so the summer journey back to known ground begins. Nanu stands and sniffs. The cubs follow suit, first Kingu and then Sivu—one, two, three in a row—tall, medium and short, forelegs at their sides, sniffing vigorously and exposing the inner part of their lips to the air to get an even better read on scents in play. The cubs have a bigger repertoire of senses now. Today, two-legged smells. And soon, two-legged sounds in the distance. As they near this unknown town, the moans of a diesel generator rise and fall on the wind.

Wanting to keep well away from the noise, but knowing from her experience around the two-legged ones in Churchill that there might be scraps to be had here as well, Nanu leads the cubs on an arc around the smell, ensuring lots of safe ground between their position and the scatter of little colored roofs with stacks spewing threads of thin smoke into the northern air. Working her way up a river, away from the community, she shows the cubs how to bathe in freshwater sloughs and roll in mud and sand to continue to clean their fur.

When it comes time to ford the river, there is nothing to be done but wade in and call to the cubs to follow. As soon as they enter the water, Kingu starts to fall behind, bleating plaintively as if the feel of the cold water has somehow released a nasty memory of oil and exhaustion. The remnants of spring ice still carom down the river, and he does his best to choose the biggest chunk he can find, but he ends up being swept farther downstream. It is Nanu's turn to bleat as she encourages Sivu through the last part of their crossing. Mother and daughter race along the far bank of the river trying to keep pace with Kingu as he whisks along, struggling to get himself out of the water and onto the ice pan.

The river has swept Kingu much closer to the community than Nanu would like. She and Sivu can see plainly a number of houses on gravel roads. They are moving inside the margin of safety that Nanu normally sets. But move to him they must. By the time the two females recross the river and catch up with him, Kingu is out of the water and digging madly among wooden crosses and little picket fences on a beach ridge over-looking the town.

Suddenly there are shouts from the village—"Wabusk, wabusk!"—followed by the sounds of machines firing up and getting louder as they roar in the direction of the bears. Nanu frantically clicks her teeth, grunts to mobilize the cubs, and the three of them run back toward the river.

Were it not for the crazy patterning of spring meltwater ponds, lingering snowdrifts and open creeks that the bears scramble over with relative ease, those in pursuit might catch up with them. Fortunately, all the bears hear is a couple of loud bangs in the distance as they run until they can run no more. Time to slow down and rest.

Whatever Nanu might know instinctively about location and direction of travel, she is on new ground here, having been swept by this year's spring storm east along the southern coast of Hudson Bay to the outskirts of the Cree community of Fort Severn. In this location, the midday sun plays more on her side than her rump. The look and smell of the community they have just skirted is different from the only other place she knew, which was bigger and nearer the open waters of Hudson Bay.

And yet there is a faint familiarity in the turning of the sun by day and the stars by night, the rhythm of the tides, the look of the remaining ice over the tidal flats and the tapering of the trees as the bears make their way along the shore.

For the cubs, it is all new. This walk and all of its sensations will linger with them for the rest of their lives.

—

The bears set up a comfortable travel rhythm, active through the early morning and late evening, when it is cool and movement requires the least amount of energy. They generally rest or sleep through the nights, which are getting longer and longer as the sun moves north, and through the middle hours of the day when the sun is highest and strongest.

As summer blooms, mosquitoes, black flies, sand midges and other biting flies hatch in waves, often making it impossible to sleep where there is no wind. So Nanu chooses places to rest that are higher, windier, like the crest of beach ridges, where there is more likelihood of keeping some of the flies at bay. Hours of light shorten by a few minutes each day, reminding Nanu that winter is on its way, and again, they will return to the hunt.

Always, though, she is on guard for her cubs, sleeping soundly for short periods but with her nose and ears attuned to any threats that might be coming their way. The cubs keep growing in size and stature. They wander farther away from their mother as she moves up the shore, and keeping track of them becomes a challenge. When she loses sight of the cubs she always calls them back.

Today, Nanu and Sivu ramble along a ridge of gravel well back from the beach. Kingu, who loves to chase crabs and worms in the shallow waters over the mud flats as the tide ebbs and flows, is, as usual, not paying much attention to where he is. As he splashes in the shallow water, his white coat is covered with ruddy foreshore mud; he has followed the receding tide and is now a speck in Nanu's visual field. Suddenly she bounds toward the shore, driven by a mother's sixth sense of danger.

Kingu is playing among the last of the winter ice pans stranded on the tidal flats. When the white top of one of these pans starts to move, he yelps with surprise. A massive male polar bear suddenly lunges at him, as if he were a seal. Kingu runs for his life with the big boar in pursuit.

Kingu is roaring, all tongue and teeth, running with every muscle fiber he can muster to the cause. When his mother gallops into sight, his pursuer veers away angrily, leaving the three of them panting and filled with adrenaline. Nanu takes little time to escort both her cubs straight inland before turning again—lesson learned—to follow the shore from a safe distance.

Throughout the heat of summer, Nanu tries to show the cubs how to save energy, but Sivu and Kingu are forever sparring, playing tug-of-war with beach flotsam, harassing birds or, in turn, being harassed by birds whose territories they inadvertently stumble into on their rambles.

One day they are drawn to movement on the sunny side of a gravel beach ridge that turns out to be their friend from the ice: the fox, in summer pelage, raising a brood of five kits. As if confused about whether the fox is friend or foe, Kingu cannot decide if he should eat them or play with them. But, on the wise counsel of their mother, the young foxes retreat to the safety of their den, whose narrow opening prevents the young boar from reaching them. Kingu moves on to the next thing that catches his eye, knowing that when hunger really strikes him, he can always return to his mother.

The cubs still tire when Nanu is on the move, but now she only travels two or so miles a day. Sivu and Kingu are now 77 and nearly 120 pounds respectively. Still they act like babies, piling onto their mother, sleeping on top of her head or draping themselves across her back.

With this rhythm of travel, the cubs grow stronger as the nights continue to become longer and the rotating stars and planets reflect from pools of still water near their sleeping nooks. They sleep as if they are one body. Occasionally, someone twitches or a stomach gurgles. Then an elbow or back leg is shifted and everyone goes back to sleep.

As August rolls into September, they have covered over 185 miles and are closer to the home range, south of Churchill. Tiny blossoms on hardy ground-hugging plants turn into berries so juicy that they stain the bears' faces and fur. Sivu and Kingu gorge themselves before rolling over and falling asleep mid-feast. By degrees, when the frost returns with the crystalline fresh cold of autumnal nights, the quiet rising of the harvest moon burnishes the entire landscape, from tawny greens to a fiery rainbow of yellows, oranges and reds. The bears' hollow guard hairs absorb the golden hues, so they blend as well on land as they do on the stark white of winter ice.

At last, after a full summer of movement along the coast, they reach known ground. Nanu knows that as they approach the time of year when they will return to the ice, there will be more potential threats afoot. Enemies can come on the land, the ice, even out of the sky. Life could change in a moment.

—

On certain days, the bears start to hear an unusual sound. Not the whine of a machine, the crack of a gun or shouts of two-legs. Today, the thump increases in volume and intensity as the whirring machine goes from a dot in the distance to a white-and-red dragonfly zooming right overhead. The cubs skitter with fear.

Nanu gathers them up and heads for cover in thick alders to hunker down and wait until the sound disappears. But the machine turns and the thump returns, increasing in intensity. It is difficult for her to separate its sound from the frantic beating of her own heart. She crouches low in the thick bushes until the thump is replaced by the roar of the engines hovering not more than ten yards overhead. She screams and the three of them make a run for it.

Should Nanu run from the threat or stand and fight? She ramps up her speed to fifteen miles per hour, running for her life. She zigs first in one direction, then zags behind a rock to see if she can make it go away. This is all new. She is afraid for her own safety but doubly worried for the safety of her young. The cubs try to follow but end up falling behind. She does her best to draw the threat away, but the cubs watch as the machine hovers overhead and just behind their mother.

The door slides open as the machine settles on a low course less than ten yards off the ground and ten yards from the running female. A rifle barrel appears. Nanu's gait breaks and she stumbles momentarily when something slams into her left shoulder. The helicopter gains altitude and wheels away the moment it is clear that the shot has hit home.

Nanu runs on for several minutes before she falters and falls onto her knees. She cannot move. By the time the cubs catch up, she is lying on her front, completely out of breath, her head still up and her eyes wide open.

They bite and poke her but she is devoid of the comforting sounds and movements that they have come to expect.

Climbing over her, they sniff the red wool flashes on a dart embedded in their mother's shoulder before backing away. They take turns licking her face to see if they can rouse her.

The sound approaches again. This time, the machine sets down on the ground beside them. Four two-legs hop out, one with a small case and one with a noose on the end of a pole. A young one, looking wide-eyed at seeing this all unfold for the first time, watches as the older man slips the noose over Nanu's head while the other begins her work. The fourth two-leg, an Inuk with a gun, stands guard nearby.

Sivu bristles and bares her teeth, so she, too, is captured and given a light dose of tranquilizer. Kingu, on the other hand, even though he is bigger, allows himself to be handled well enough. Like Sivu, he is weighed and measured and given an ear tag, then he retires to a distance just out of reach as the scientists move on to gather information from his mother.

In less than thirty minutes, the work is done and the machine sound fades into the distance, leaving the cubs clambering over their mother in a swirl of turbine exhaust. They work around her as she struggles to sit up, sorting through smells of anesthetic, antiseptic and blood. They pull on the new collar but finally make their way around her body to access the familiar comforts of her belly and begin to nurse.

—

Heading back to their camp near Churchill, the science team is pleased with what they have accomplished. With their young Inuit summer research assistant who has just that much more vocational experience as a result of this field foray, they have captured, logged and collared another healthy female bear and two new cubs of the year. So many things can go wrong, but they have correctly estimated the sow's weight by sight and given her only enough tranquilizer to let them gather their data, and no more. And the cubs cooperated. It doesn't always go like that.

While she was anesthetized, the lead hand used a sterile scalpel to nick the skin so that the barb on the dart could be released. The other examined Nanu to assess her general health and body condition and to ensure that the process of apprehending her has not caused any damage. Next they used dental pliers to remove a vestigial molar just behind her lower canine tooth to determine her age. While this was going on, the other scientist prepared tattoo pliers with indelible ink to apply a permanent number to Nanu's inside upper lip. Ear tags were next. Like a series of well-practiced dance steps, the whole process took only five minutes.

Next were tissue sampling and body measurements. Rolling Nanu onto a net with the help of the Inuit assistant who put down his shotgun just long enough to help move the bear, they accessed her inner thigh and took several tubes of blood for further analysis before hoisting her with a pulley system to determine her exact weight with a spring scale. Quick tape measure of girth and nose to tail length allowed those values to be entered in the new record.

By this point in the capture process, Nanu's eyes are starting to move. Sivu is coming around as well, rolling back her lips and sniffing reflexively. She can smell her mother's blood. As the pilot starts up the helicopter again, the final sample is a few hairs snipped, bagged and numbered from all three, along with a needle biopsy of subcutaneous fat on Sivu and Nanu. These tissue samples will be frozen and archived for future research, but in the immediate instance, back at the lab, they will be analyzed to develop a full picture of persistent pollutants, heavy metals and other contaminants.

Sivu's light dose of tranquilizer has completely worn off, and she starts calling plaintively to her mother. Nanu turns her head toward the sound. While one scientist steadies her head, the other hurriedly packs up all their things and runs back to the helicopter. She returns with a box containing a smooth white collar that they affix to Nanu's neck. In the early days, these collars would be tracked by scientists in nearby aircraft, but now, with the honing of sophisticated microdigital technology, bears can be tracked year-round by satellite, allowing scientists to match location with landform and vegetation types when on land and to determine where the bears are and how far and how fast they move on the ice or in the water. At first, because of the thick, strong necks of male bears, which allowed them to shed a collar easily, only females could be successfully tracked in this way. Now, however, ear tags—more sophisticated than the ones assigned to Sivu and Kingu with their capture—have even smaller geo-positioning transmitters and long-lasting lithium batteries, which allow adult males to be tracked for months as well. This positioning data from capture and tracking has been essential over the years for plotting range size, seasonal movements, and year-over-year hunting and reproductive success, among other parameters of bear habit and behavior.

eight
Independence

ᔅᖂᕿᕝ ᓄᒐᐊᖅᑕᐅᔪ ᐅᖁᔭᕐᓂ

Freeze Up Moon

OCTOBER

—

Over the eight years of her life so far, Nanu has learned that ice, on fresh and saltwater, can be surprising. From autumns spent rambling along this coast, during two of which she was pregnant, waiting for winter, she knows that darkness fills her world like a dark liquid as the season progresses. The temperature drops, freshwater ponds and puddles on the land become solid, and snow falls. Yet the salt water of Hudson Bay has a mind of its own.

When it finally does relent to winter, it skins over, leaving skirts of ice around boulders on the foreshore with each tide cycle. When the tide rises again, new ice sinks through the runoff-rich fresher water at the surface, leaving a thick slurry of ice and water that swirls back and forth, sometimes for weeks through wicked autumn weather. After months of fasting and living on grasses and berries, bears can wait end-lessly for solid ice to form.

Nanu, of course, has learned that the currents of the Hud-son Bay gyre circle counterclockwise, from left to right in the southern half of the bay. Ice here always moves toward the rising sun. She has also learned through experience that the possibil-ity of actually walking on the surface of Hudson Bay increases only when pans of broken floes that have formed farther north cycle down and start to coalesce into hard surfaces that can sup-port the full weight of a bear.

This year, as Sivu and Kingu spar with other cubs along the shore, she minds from a distance. Like the other mothers, she vocalizes warnings when big males move through the nursery. All of the bears are essentially moving en masse toward the bay for when the ice starts to solidify, but in the meantime, squab-bles can break out. Finally, by the light of a full moon flaring through the first full winter auroras, Nanu decides it is time to move her family.

Stepping out onto the new ice, Nanu relaxes so that her forelegs slide, like runners on a sled, to distribute her weight over a larger surface area. The cubs follow along behind. The ice is almost springy, bending under Nanu's weight but not breaking. The cubs slide toward her on the depression that forms around her in the surface of the ice. But soon the ice starts to fracture with tiny cracks and the depression around her starts to fill with water. It isn't long before she and the cubs are quite wet. The young ones retreat to shore.

Suddenly Nanu's body breaks through the ice altogether, immersing her head, collar and shoulders in the dark water below. As she tries to scramble back to the surface of the ice, her rump is immersed as well. As much as she tries to bring her forepaws back onto the surface of the ice, it breaks again and again. Finally, she begins breaking a path back to shore, where the cubs watch patiently. They dance around as their mother eventually clambers back up onto landfast ice, sniffing the air all the while.

That evening, the air pressure drops, ushering in a storm from the south that slowly increases in intensity. The temperature rises to near the freezing point, and all they can do is to find another hollow well back from the beach to wait it out. By morning, everything, including the trio, is covered with a thick blanket of fresh soft snow.

A yawning lead of black water has formed between the shore and the floes that had looked so promising the previous day. They watch as this gap of open water widens with the continuing pressure of the offshore wind. And that force, along with the insistent urging of the counterclockwise gyre, keeps increasing the distance between shore and the receding floes. Suddenly Hudson Bay is wide open again.

Shorter days and gnawing hunger remind Nanu of the obvious. It is long past time to return to the ice. But the scene before them looks more like early than late autumn. Had she had even one more week of hunting before their hasty exit from the ice in the spring, she would have been in better shape now. The shorter season on the ice is now a fact of their lives. She must persevere. Or die.

Waiting is something Nanu is used to, as are all the bears from Svalbard to Siberia and around the circumpolar world. They can pick at kelp on the beach or scrounge for carrion to keep the cubs busy. And the cubs can nurse to keep their nutrition and growth going. But she needs to make an assessment of where the ice that had formed has gone.

To gain perspective, she heads away from the beach to a gravel ridge some distance away, above Sivu and Kingu. She stands on the ridge looking out across the open water. Is it a mirage, or is there ice out there? For better or worse, they head back to the shore. Nanu wades into the water at high tide, encouraging her almost-a-year-old twins to follow. Together they begin swimming toward ice she cannot see but hopes is there.

Kingu has never been the same since the oil incident in the spring. His urine has a funny smell. He is always hungry, but he tires quickly, even though he is in fair physical condition. Sivu is in better shape than her brother. And together they have more body mass, more fat under their skin (although less than they might have had). They are also much more accomplished and energy-efficient swimmers. The three of them move smoothly through the water. How long it will take to reach the ice is uncertain, but Nanu has committed to taking the chance.

After several hours of making good progress in the water, they startle a seal that races between them. It wheels around, dives, and then surfaces again just ahead of them, unusual behavior for a seal. It squawks, takes a quick breath, and then races between them again. Before Kingu can turn to give chase, their attention is drawn to strange black triangles in the water approaching at high speed.

Nanu dives for a better look. The cubs do the same but pop right back up, unable to hold their breath for as long as their mother. These new creatures look something like beluga whales, but they are bigger. And they are mostly black instead of white and gray—black with white markings.

The three bears watch as the whales dive and rip below, leaving them buffeted by the underwater currents of flukes and pectoral fins powering by.

In response to the threat, Kingu and Nanu dive deeper to swim away from the whales. But Sivu takes a slap of an unexpected wave and must cough to clear the water from her windpipe. That is all it takes to separate the three. In less than a minute, the whales are back, this time approaching from the left, moving quickly at the surface in a formation that creates a substantial and very intentional wave. Their target is Sivu.

Her fearful bleat is swallowed by the wave as the whales roar past. She rises a few feet up in the water, her shoulders entering the air with the force of the wave hitting her, then she disappears. The bears can do nothing other than turn and watch her disappear.

Sivu surfaces again to catch her breath, now bawling to her mother, just in time to see the whales coming at her from the opposite direction. This time she is ready and holds her breath as the wave sweeps her up in the water and back down. And a third attack, from the rear, exhausts her. She is sputtering but still moving under her own power.

Suddenly one of the smaller orcas surfaces in front of her, her dorsal fin nearly touching Sivu's paddling front feet, and breaches right in front—almost *on*—the young bear. Nanu, with Kingu not far behind, turns to fight. But it is like nothing they have ever encountered before.

The next tail smack is a direct hit on Sivu, knocking her unconscious. She slowly starts to sink, leaving a trail of her own bubbles. Nanu dives to try to push her daughter back to the surface, but by now, Sivu is heavy and unresponsive. Nanu circles and dives, dives and circles.

Below, Sivu is suspended motionless in a wash of indigo, like the night sky, tiny bubbles of air rising out of her mouth and coat, like stars in a different heaven.

—

Nanu and Kingu swim on and eventually reach the floe edge. Kingu, who by now is very cold, drags himself out and latches onto his mother to feed, as he has not done for many hours.

By now, Kingu is approaching 220 pounds, about half his mother's weight. His grizzly-like cub's face has matured, the long bones of his legs have lengthened. He is still a recognizably smaller animal than his mother, but in the coming year, if they are able to get the necessary nutrition, he will grow as tall as his mother. But to do that, they need to eat.

Unfortunately, seals on new ice are more dispersed and harder to catch. And thin ice transmits news of a bear's presence near an aglu in plenty of time for a seal to escape. Edges of forming floes offer much easier places to feed. And newly formed ice is smoother, with fewer places to haul out seals. The smells on the breeze diminish with fewer kills. And there are fewer ravens in the sky or foxes tripping along in the shadows. On early ice, successful hunting is as much a matter of luck as it is of experience.

With his sister gone, Kingu stays closer to Nanu than he might otherwise have done. And yet, as a maturing adult, he is exploring the crystalline world in every direction. Normally, they hunt mostly in the early-morning and late-evening hours, but with days only six hours long and with ever-present hunger driving Nanu onward, they are prowling more than they are sleeping. Kingu is definitely more interested in the hunt. When his mother urges him on, he will follow, often putting some distance between them so that they investigate a broader territory for seal traces of any kind.

Kingu's senses, too, are getting sharper by the day. Any movement, any vibration in the ice, any whiff, any sound that comes his way is taken in and processed. Still, he always checks what his mother is doing. Without his sister, there is just his mother for companionship and direction, and when she is hunting, she has no tolerance for foolery. Kingu knows the satisfactions of fresh seal now. He has a clear idea of what they are looking for. His attention span has increased as well.

Early one morning, while his mother is still sleeping, Kingu happens to find two gulls who have flown out from the river estuaries at Churchill in search of the pickings of successful bear hunts. Through the darkest part of the night, they, too, had stopped to rest. With one foot tucked up in the downy underfeathers of their bellies, their other foot had frozen to an overflow near a crack in the ice. One gull had been able to extricate himself and get into the air, but the other had been less fortunate. Kingu had stalked it, and to his surprise, expecting it, too, to rise away and laugh at him, he landed on the bird. The first meal of his own making that second winter on the ice was feathers and fishy-tasting bird meat. If adult female bears could experience pride, then that is exactly what Nanu might have felt when her young boar trotted up that morning with a bedraggled gull wing in his mouth.

Smelling fresh meat, even if it is a mostly consumed gull, only intensifies the hunger Nanu is experiencing as their first hours on the ice turn into days and weeks. True, she went without food the previous winter, when she denned and the cubs were born. But she is now moving from six to seven months without proper nutrition.

Patience and perseverance eventually deliver and Nanu lands a big male bearded seal, who is almost too big and strong for her to handle now. Kingu, knowing that the first meal of the seal belongs to the hunter, hangs back while his mother feasts. He has learned that his approach to the kill must be from the side, where he licks his mother's greasy mouth to indicate his readiness to join the meal.

They eat to the point where another mouthful will simply not fit in their stomachs. Nanu has consumed nearly 130 pounds of fat, and Kingu, a quarter of that. Then they roll into the family heap and sleep, but not for long because they are both awakened by a wind shift that brings to them the distinctive smell of a big boar, who has circled downwind from miles away.

In a lean season for seals, a male is working his way up the vapor trail to see what meal might be had. Had the wind not changed and Nanu not sensed his approach, he might have come upon them. Nanu clicks her teeth and chuffs quickly to mobilize her cub, and the two of them retreat to a safe distance from the remains of the seal while the intruder has his fill. By the time they circle back, drawn by the fluster of ravens arguing with a fox over the leavings, all that remains of the seal is bones, gristle and a well-picked skeleton.

And that is the way the winter goes. As the ice matures,

they move into the seal-pupping moons of winter. There seems to be lots of available habitat, and there are definitely signs of seals that attract Kingu's attention, but success is not on their side. Instead of one kill in twenty tries, Nanu's average is more like one in thirty tries. As the sun rises into the winter sky, again pooling meltwater ponds on the ice, Nanu has gained less than half the weight that she needs to see her easily through another summer fast.

The good news is that the fat content of her milk has gradually decreased, and its production is making much lower demands on her energy. Kingu is nursing less as he is getting more and more calories from prey. But Nanu needs to consume enough calories to build up at least a minimal fat reserve. The ice is decaying. The sky is again alive with birds. Time is running out.

This season, Nanu and Kingu have had to move farther north and west than they had the previous season. As the ice decays behind them, Nanu keeps moving forward with the expectation of better hunting ahead, always moving until the surface of the ice becomes too fractured to continue. But the hunting docs not improve. Kingu manages to stalk and kill a late-season whitecoat, which he shares with Nanu. She joins the subsequent stakeout on the broken lair, but the mother seal never appears.

With the advance of winter, a wide-open lead along the western shore of the big bay opens. Nanu, Kingu and the other bears in the area can smell something besides open water on the wind. It is not the smell of seals but of whales. One of the spring's first pods of beluga whales is on its customary way down from open ocean farther north, heading toward the big river estuaries. The whales navigate through the pack ice at the edge of the floe, breathing comfortably as they fish the waters below. But a chance quick freeze catches them too far away to make a run to the floe edge. To stay alive, a couple dozen of them are forced into one place in the ice, creating a small opening—or "sassat"—where they take turns surfacing to breathe.

Nanu and Kingu work their way toward the busy pool, drawn by the smell of blood. They soon see a massive boar flailing from the edge of the hole. In the bloodred water are the raked and ragged backs of trapped belugas. As they arrive, the boar dives on top of one of the smaller whales, savagely biting at its blowhole. The sheer weight of the bear takes them both under the water. It is a life-and-death tangle. Other whales in the pod, desperate for a breath, surface above them. But somehow the two separate, the whale escapes, and the big boar explodes through the maelstrom of red and white and back onto the ice.

Kingu takes up a vigil at the edge, swiping at belugas as they arch for breath. Nanu watches from behind. The large boar is more intent than ever. A strategic hunter, he is watching for the animal whose blowhole he had damaged on his last dive. Another pounce is enough to subdue the injured whale, who is probably drowning in its own blood. Kingu flails toward the action as other big males elbow in as well. With the whale nearly incapable of further movement, the big boar is able to grab it sufficiently to drag it to the edge of the hole. Nanu and other bears join in to haul the animal onto the ice, where the feast begins. Nanu and Kingu take their turns when the bigger animals have had their fill. It will be a last substantial meal before the ice lets go.

The weather warms. The remainder of white whales escape. And the bears, slimmer this year, head back to shore to begin another summer fast.

—

As the scientists watch the data stream in from Nanu's satellite collar, they know she is heading for the shoreline. What the collar does not reveal is what she weighs now. Nor does it indicate that she has lost one cub, as the ear tags do not have satellite capabilities. They know only that she is moving in ever-widening arcs on the ice in the hope of catching one last seal before leaving the ice and facing head-on the many pressures of yet another summer fast in what is becoming a struggle to survive.

nine
Rebirth

ᖃᐅᒪᑦᑖᖅᖠᖅ

The Sun Gets Higher

FEBRUARY

—

This time, Kingu and Nanu come ashore onto familiar ground just north of Churchill, near the site of the original Hudson's Bay Company post at the estuary of the Nelson and Hayes Rivers. The taste and smell of the freshening water, the vapors of emerging spring earth, the essence of spruce on the wind are familiar. Although they leave the ice within sight of other bears, they aren't visible long on tidal flats before they are swallowed by the monochromatic landscape of awakening tundra greens.

Kingu is not quite as tall as his mother, but even in this lean season his steady diet of milk has allowed him to grow to 330 pounds and to be better prepared than his mother for his second summer fast. Happily for him, mother's milk can still feed a yearling as another summer on the land begins.

But Nanu weighs only 500 pounds. Less than two years ago, she weighed 770 pounds. With every passing day, her energy resources diminish, and her body mass declines.

This second summer ashore will be a time to continue her teachings, particularly about walking hibernation and ways to conserve energy through the summer fast. After eighteen months, Kingu and his mother make their way without even having to look where the other might be.

By August, the heat of summer has passed. Cool nights return. Moving north, they recross the swift-flowing waters of both the Hayes and Nelson Rivers but not before checking water pools orphaned by tides for landlocked river fish or salt-water species like Arctic char that have come upstream from Hudson Bay. Drawn by the ravens and occasionally by bald eagles cruising the river updrafts, or following the scents of otters who will lead them along the muddy cutbanks of the rivers to fish, they nibble on scavengings, some fresher than others. Some fish are still alive and catchable in shallow water. There is abundant freshwater to help digest the protein, but calorically, the fat content of fish, compared to seal, is hardly worth the effort. Still, it gives the pair something to do as they amble and sleep their way back to the best place to wait for new ice.

Tundra ponds reflect back the clear autumn skies until ice crystals mute colors into a kaleidoscope of change. Lengthening nights fade into the phosphorescent glow of the harvest moon. Stars rotate behind the returning auroras. The bears wait. Watch. And wait again.

With another summer of foraging over gravel and mud and open tundra behind them, they have both finished their annual molt. The summer dirt is gone, but their new coats are tinged with gold as much as white, particularly when the sun is low to the horizon. As the weather cools, their fur thickens, they sleep less and a certain restlessness comes over them. Soon they will return to the ice, to the seals, to other bears. This year, they will follow trails Nanu knows they have walked before.

As the sun crosses the equator at the September equinox, a constant low hum and the sound of occasional machines overhead and machines on the tundra remind Nanu that their world has other occupants. Nanu is inclined to move farther inland, knowing it will be some time yet before the bayside vigil for ice should begin. Kingu, for whatever reason, heads toward the noise. Nanu follows reluctantly.

In the distance, they see a commotion of moving shapes on the green. The shapes, following in line, are moving slowly toward them. As these strange vehicles approach, Kingu stands up to see and sniff and listen. Just as Nanu signals it is time to run, the movement and the noise suddenly stop.

Looking to his mother for cues, Kingu senses that she is curious, too. He moves a little closer. Nanu follows. And closer. Before they actually see the two-legs, they can smell and sense them. But there seems to be no threat here.

The two of them make their way toward the tundra buggy as it lumbers to a stop. From inside, there is the constant patter of camera shutters and low screams of delight as the bears clamber onto the tundra tires and stand with their faces closer to the windows. A small two-leg places his hand on the glass.

—

Finally, within just weeks of Kingu's second birthday, under a moonless sky so clear that the usual guiding constellations fade within the gauzy depths of the Milky Way, a deep cold front rolls through. The temperature plummets. From their vantage point on the shore, Kingu and Nanu watch as ice crystals form at the surface and sink, but not before they grow tendrils of ice that bind into networks that solidify the bay. The low sun rises and reflects from this new surface with blinding intensity. Still, they wait.

But with another day and night and day passing, crystals like miniature conifers start to form on the surface of the new ice. By now, even Kingu knows that the ice, coming down from the north on the currents of Hudson Bay, is what they need to see and where they need to head. Early in the season, this is where the surface of the bay is most solid, but it is also where the possibility of quick hunting success is highest. As the earth spins toward the solstice, with most of the other bears either ahead or behind them, they crunch their way due north in a fan pattern of prints. With the energy, vapors and sounds of the land falling behind them, Kingu and Nanu retune their senses to one thing. Seals.

Kingu has been nursing almost constantly over these last days of the freeze-up vigil. Nanu has pushed him away, but he is no longer a cub and takes what he wants. Yet, as they leave the snow-dusted land behind them, Kingu is more focused on the hunt than anything else. They choose to walk half a mile apart, widening their search. When it is time to rest, Kingu finds his way back closer to his mother, whose presence is still comforting.

It is Kingu who gets lucky early on in a stationary hunt on

the smooth ice of early winter. No one is more surprised than the young bear himself when he crunches down on a careless bearded seal so massive he must break ice around the aglu with his front paws to bring it up on the ice. By the time he has opened its belly and taken his first gorging mouthfuls of warm summer fat, Nanu is on the scene. He moves to accommodate her feeding on the carcass, but the pair of them bristle and make growling noises when another sow and cub arrive. This is not a kill they are prepared to share, at least not until they have had their fill. By the time they doze off beside the kill, the other bears have moved on. The raven is picking. The fox, too, has furtively found her way to a first winter feed.

As winter sets in, Kingu stops nursing altogether. He spends more and more time alone, hunting in the early morning hours, sleeping, moving on his own arc, now the center of his own universe.

The pair drift slowly apart. If he knows, or senses, where his mother is, west of him along the west Hudson Bay shore lead, it is of nearly no consequence to him. At twenty-seven months old he is on his own, not mature enough to breed for a few more years to come but certainly skilled and competent enough, with luck on his side, to make his own way in the world. Nanu, for her part, now nine years old and readying for another turn of her life cycle, wastes no time in finally drying up her milk supply. And with that change come the stirrings that will start her reproductive cycle anew. Soon there will be indications of her impending readiness to mate in every breath she takes, every track she makes.

—

And so the winter passes. Many seals are hunted and consumed. But increasingly, with each meal, the chemicals of faraway industrial processes are passed through the chain of life to the bears. Polychlorinated biphenyl. PCBs. These chemicals likely built up in Kingu's would-be sire, the scarred old boar, and could have played a role in his failed attempt to mate with Nanu. Perhaps Kingu will avoid a similar fate. But that is the risk a predator at the top of the food chain faces.

The spring equinox brings days and nights of equal length, marking the halfway point on the march toward twenty-four hour sun. Ravens, foxes and bears now regularly get wind of two-legs from the Inuit communities, like Arviat and Tikirarjuaq, on the western shores of Hudson Bay hunting for seals. If the opportunity presents itself, there might be a bear to be taken as well.

Today, Kingu's ears prick to the faraway moans of snow machines. Occasionally, with the tricks that the wind and air of different temperatures can play, distant sounds seem strangely near over the ice. The machine smells wend their way from the west. They speak of goings-on beyond a world he can see with his eyes and ears. He has lived long enough to know that he shares a world of ice not only with the raven and the fox and the first spring birds—and other bears, of course—but also with the two-leg.

Yet Kingu revels in a bumper year for seals. His stomach is so full at times, and the temperatures so high, that he must pant to stay cool in this frozen world. He gets more round with every kill. Sometimes, he takes a whitecoat just because he can, more for sport than anything else. But he has learned that there is possible reward in that, too. Even with the absence of a pup and the smell of blood and bears around an aglu, a female seal will persist, calling and looking for the pup. Kingu cannot resist another meal.

Nanu has a different path to take. Every footprint she makes leaves visual evidence of her passing for anyone who might care to follow. From glands in black pads of her well-furred feet come again a chemical signature that speaks of her physiological state, her general health, her readiness to mate. The circling has begun anew.

A couple of days behind on the ice are two boars who will continue to follow Nanu's tracks until they collide in the mating contest. But much closer and moving much faster is a suitor of a different sort, on a snowmobile, moving upwind, so the sounds and smells of the machine and its driver fall behind. He has picked up Nanu's tracks in a skiff of new spring snow. Huddled among caribou hides in a qamutiik, strung out on a long line behind, are two young children and their mother, food, tent, Coleman stove, fuel and camping supplies, and three short-legged Inuit dogs.

When Nanu hears their approach in the distance, instinct makes her circle back to gain downwind advantage so that she can more fully explore the possible threat. Conveniently, a pressure ridge serves to mask this maneuver. As she stands in a place where she can look back across the bright open ice, the noise stops and she sees a two-legged one, standing on top of his machine, hands to his eyes. She catches a whiff of the exhaust, the people and the dogs. Dogs. Not good.

She drops down again on all fours and moves quickly into

the broken ice of the ridge, eventually finding a place where she can hide under a cantilevered ice shelf, and out of view until they pass.

The machine sound starts again. She lies out of sight waiting for that moment, as she has learned to do with machines approaching overhead. She waits. The machine sound reaches a crescendo and then starts to diminish, but it is just a trick of the wind. The sound starts to reverberate in her body. Through the drone, she hears children yelling and dogs barking. The motor sound drops again but the barking continues. The dogs now move toward her.

They cross the pressure ridge on the exact trail she had followed just minutes before, yelping at a fever pitch to let the hunter know they are nearly there, at the end of the search. She hears their feet scratching to make their way through the broken ice planes in the ridge. When she hears their breathing with their barking, she extracts herself from this temporary lair and makes a run for open ice. It is her last option.

The sound of the dogs is enough to let the hunter know that they are in direct pursuit. The machine roars back to life. Nanu hears it flanking her to get out in front. The dogs are behind. The last of the pressure ridge is beside her.

Suddenly they are all out on open ice, running in the same direction, dogs fanning out to both sides. The machine, having fallen back, is now running less than a hundred yards behind her, obliterating her track. Running full speed, she stops, looks over her shoulder to see the hunter. He has detached the qamutiik and is now standing on his machine instructing the dogs to close in. The machine roars. Nanu runs on.

She is feeling winded, but it is the heat of exertion building up inside of her that starts slowing her down. The machine slows and stops, leaving the dogs to follow at a safe distance. As she feels the heat building up inside her even more, she breaks to a slow canter, then a trot and then to a fast walk that is still no match for the dogs, who, though out of shape from eleven months on chains, look as if they are only mildly exercised. Eventually, panting now from heat and exertion, she stops and splays all fours on the snow, putting her hot and thinning underside into direct contact with the ice.

Two dogs lie down on either side of her. The third circles around in front and sits, close enough for her to see the yellow in his eyes. The machine is moving again and circles near. The engine stops. She hears the clatter of steel on steel as a round is chambered and the rifle bolt cocked. Then, mixed with the sound of hcr own labored breathing, she hears a sure succession of slow footsteps crunching in the snow.

Bear. Dogs. Hunter.

Miles away to the east, Kingu hears the crack and stops what he is doing.

—

Farther away, the scientists tracking Nanu will know that this moment was the end of the visible data stream for this female bear, either through an alert in the telemetry data recording or by receiving her collar returned through the mail by the hunter.

—

For the Inuk hunter, this day is just the next in a ten-thousand-year succession of days that have come and gone since humans left the land and made their way onto the ice and into a living partnership with the snow and water, with the seals and ice and ravens, with the air and its winds of change, and with the bears of all creation. In the pause before he pulls a small knife from a beautifully sewn sealskin scabbard hanging from the handlebars of his snow machine, he stands still over the bear, his eyes closed momentarily. Every hunter does this differently, but in this moment of thanks is a sacred reflection in the here and now. More significantly, there is also a prayer acknowledging the infinite sphere of mutuality that nourishes and sustains both people and bears.

—

Days later, under cover of the twilight of impending summer, Kingu comes across a single blood-soaked mitten on the snow at the end of a line of tracks leading away from a nearby pressure ridge. All around, in the air, on the ice, in the energy swirling still around the place, he can hear and feel and sense his mother.

Overhead, in the darkening sky, hangs a crescent moon. Kingu looks up. Nanu will guide him, just as surely as she had guided him on this ice, just as surely as polar bears have guided their young for two hundred thousand years. And so he walks on alone, as long as the ice will last.

afterword
An Arctic World in Peril

n her ten years roaming the lands and waters of southwestern Hudson Bay, Nanu, like other bears throughout the circumpolar world, encountered and responded to a host of challenges that can be directly or indirectly tracked back to climate change. Her failed first pregnancy could have been caused by a number of factors, but science has established that if a female doesn't have the energy resources to sustain a pregnancy—in other words, if she came ashore that autumn without sufficient fat on her body to make it through the winter because the hunting season was too short or seal-hunting success was low for whatever reason—this can decrease reproductive success.

And then there is the litany of factors, any one of which on its own is unlikely to cause mortality or to have a significant effect but all of which act cumulatively when other stresses are added: later freeze-up, earlier breakup (shorter winters, longer summers); forest fires on the tundra; shifting seal-population dynamics; winter lightning and other unusual weather effects; competition with other land-based, black and brown bears; newer species, like orcas, moving in large numbers into polar bear waters; changes in snowpack, snowfall amounts, and drifting patterns; circulating aerial and aquatic pollutants; encroachment of development from industry, including increased shipping, roads, tracks and tourism. The list goes on—all things perpetrated by people and places far removed from any kind of direct contact with bears.

Science has estimated, as have Inuit elders through oral history teaching, that over the millennia polar bear populations have gone up and down, as have populations and migrations of northern people. Before the arrival of Europeans, humans and bears lived in a dynamic equilibrium that included predation, life and death. Northern people had a profound sense of respect for that balance. At no time did either threaten the other with the possibility of extirpation or total extinction. Until now.

In the early days of scientific inquiry in the Arctic, which began more or less with the arrival of the first Europeans, northern Indigenous peoples were not included in the creation of the knowledge, except perhaps peripherally as guides or hosts for the scientists. Happily, that situation began to change beginning in the last quarter of the twentieth century, to the point that now most northern wildlife populations, including polar bears, are co-managed with policies and plans based in a mix of Western and traditional scientific data. But we have a considerable distance to go to narrow the gap between the two: Western science still "rules" more often than it should in decisions about northern development.

The struggle for northern peoples, as communities evolve away from subsistence harvesting and traditional ways of life and toward a wage-based work and store-bought food, is to find ways to grow and prosper in a global economy while still maintaining an essential connection to the land and to the traditions of the land on which cultural health and wholeness is founded. For Inuit particularly, in the Russian Far East, Alaska, Greenland and Canada, connection to the land is a matter of heart and spirit, but it is also a matter of nourishing bodies and minds with the bounty of the land, which, in every kill, in every hunting tradition, in every bite, affirms who and what they are and, by proxy, who and what we are, what humanity is at its essence.

In countries like Russia, Norway and the United States, it is illegal to hunt polar bears. For Indigenous peoples of those countries whose very existence was or is totally integrated with polar bears, a prohibition on polar bear harvest is effectively a prohibition on the goal of health and cultural prosperity. To say that the rights of Indigenous peoples matter and then to deny traditional subsistence harvesting of any species is contradictory at best.

In Canada, through an evolving and responsive quota system that controls the number and sex of bears to be harvested in any given year, the co-managed bear hunt continues as a source of food and income—a source of cultural completion—for the Inuit. Those who would support this subsistence hunting policy and practice recognize that since time immemorial bears and people have shared the northern ice. Sadly, there are those who would point to the barrel of the hunter's gun and vilify the hunter when, in fact, the most significant threat to the future existence of polar bears—and to the people of the northern ice—is habitat encroachment by industry and climate change.

If climate change is caused by human appetites that have somehow lost track of the rules—the necessary and intimate connections between humans and nature—then what my forty years of northern travel have revealed is that there is timely wisdom in remembering and rekindling the knowledge we have lost to "progress." We might relearn simply by listening to those whose relationship with the nonhuman is written into the cycle of life.

To suggest that the future of polar bears should be treated as distinct from the survival of the Indigenous people who have cohabited the circumpolar world with bears since the very beginning is to deny their essential interconnection. It persists in body, mind and spirit; in language and culture; in stories and stars. We must find that balance again, if indeed it is there to be found. We might start by considering bears and people, ravens and whales, as one and the same. As such, we— all peoples, all living beings—we *are* the bear, as my northern friends have known all along.

On the page opposite is a southerly view of the late-night sky over Igloolik, Nunavut, as seen around the time of the winter solstice, but only those stars and constellations named by Iglulingmiut are shown. The Tukturjuit constellation is what the Westerners call Ursa Major, or the Big Dipper. For conventional, non-Indigenous astronomers, this constellation is our bear and she points to the North Star, and is the root concept of our word "Arctic," which comes from the Greek *arktos* or *arktikos* and means "home of the bear."

For the Inuit, though, Tukturjuit means "caribou," and it is in the constellation of Nanurjuk that they see their bear and in Qimmiit that they see the dogs referenced in the story opening this book. What fascinates me is that the bearness of Nanurjuk is invisible to Westerners even though we're looking right at it, and have been since our ancestors first started building a cosmology in the night sky and called this constellation Taurus. But Nanu has always been there, as she will continue to be for Kingu.

The Inuit star map is just one perspective; each of the polar peoples has its own cosmology. Being aware of this duality, or rather plurality, in the night sky is important to an understanding of our shared history and perhaps is a step forward to a better future, one where Inuit and non-Inuit can find their place in the sky.

An Inuit Star Map

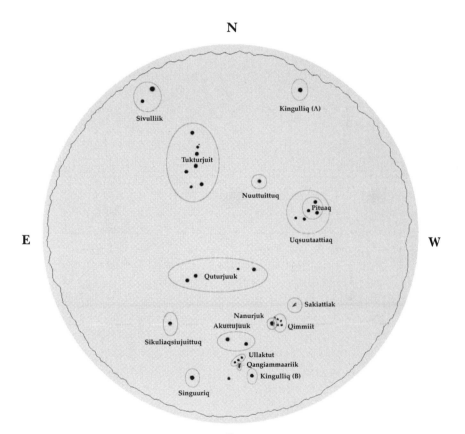

N

Sivulliik

Kingulliq (Λ)

Tukturjuit

Nuuttuittuq

Pituaq

Uqsuutaattiaq

E

W

Quturjuuk

Sakiattiak

Nanurjuk

Akuttujuuk

Qimmiit

Sikuliaqsiujuittuq

Ullaktut

Qangiammaariik

Kingulliq (B)

Singuuriq

S

Author's Note

If it seems odd that a writer who began life as a marine biologist would be stretching the bounds of creative nonfiction with a story about a made-up bear, let me explain.

In the early years of my postsecondary education, there was nothing I wanted more than to become a person of science. Back in the 1970s, as I was contemplating what I might do in graduate school, chance and almost unbelievable good fortune found me working in a university research facility.

My job was to teach an adult male polar bear to press paddles on a fancy experimental setup that had been perfected to assess the spectral sensitivity of the bear's eyes. I would shine a light of known color and intensity into the bear's eyes. If he saw the light, Huxley—he had a Canadian Wildlife Service number, but that was his name, given to him by one of my colleagues after his famous godfather, biologist Julian Huxley— would press a paddle with his nose to say "yes." If he didn't see the light, he would indicate "no" by pressing another paddle in the other direction.

Hour after hour, day after day, month after month with that magnificent animal—who was slowly going berserk in captivity—led me to leave the pursuit of natural science in a lab setting. Instead, for over forty years, I lived for part of the year among the northern peoples of Canada's Arctic, traveling to circumpolar countries, appreciating other ways of life. In Churchill, Manitoba, I had my first interaction with wild bears. This disciplinary shift from marine biology to cultural anthropology brought with it an awareness of what counts as truth and what it means to know.

Now, after more than four decades of living with and learning from Indigenous peoples throughout the circumpolar world, I have a keen sense that although science is a powerful tool, it is really just one way of appreciating our world. "Bearness," if I might call it that, has many dimensions—narrative, nutritional, cultural, psychological, visual, aural, olfactory, spiritual, experiential, linguistic, functional, geographic. From spiritual to cultural to psychological perspectives, I'm wondering if bears and people are perhaps two sides of the same ontological coin.

When I set out to portray the life cycle of a female polar bear in southwestern Hudson Bay, the challenge was to find a voice and a genre that would invite readers to explore a spectrum of ways in which humans know bears and how bears know humans. The lingering scientist in me eschewed putting words in a bear's mouth. It was important that these bears did not talk. It was also important for me to ensure that the facts of the story—the natural and cultural histories of the bear, the oceanography of the bay, the morphology and behavior of the ice, the environment of the Hudson Bay lowlands through the seasons—accurately reflected four decades of Arctic learning and experience.

All of what you have read here is "true" to the absolute best of my understanding of how polar bears and people co-exist in Arctic realms around the circumpolar world and what they are contending with—what is at stake—as their worlds are shifting in response to anthropogenic climate change. Giving the bears names, physical characteristics and personality traits—all of which are drawn from existing and available bear scholarship and lore—was my means of inviting you to engage with the story and to enter the *Ice Walker* world long enough to ponder what we are doing to the earth, what we are doing to the bears, what we are doing to ourselves, and what might be done about all of that, before the world as we know it—the world enriched by northern peoples and bears—is gone for good.

—

My friend and Inuit elder David Serkoak, who was born on the northern tip of Nueltin Lake, southwest of Arviat, Nunavut, provided the descriptions of the moons and seasons in the chapter heads, with the exception of chapter nine. That description was adapted from the Calendar of Inuit Seasons published by Tungasuvvingat Inuit, the only Inuit-specific service organization of its kind providing social support, cultural activities and frontline services to Inuit as well as advice and support on Inuit topics to other agencies across Canada, such as shelters, courts, publishers, hospitals and schools. The names of the stars are taken from John MacDonald's *The Arctic Sky: Inuit Astronomy, Star Lore, and Legend.* I have attempted to verify the spelling and grammar of all Inuit words used herein, but any errors are my own.

Photo Credits

Further Reading

Bilodeau, Chantal. 2015. *Sila: The Arctic Cycle.* Canada: Talon-books.

This dramatic play by Quebec writer and translator Chantal Bilodeau is the first production of the Arctic Cycle, a series of eight plays that examine the impact of climate change on the eight circumpolar nations. Winner of a number of national awards, the work includes parts for two polar bears who, in their non-speaking roles, help the other nine characters in the story bridge what the playwright calls the "two distinct Arctics" of north and south. This is a collaboratively derived and powerful imagining of what might be the essential significance of polar bears as symbol and foundational myth, transcending disciplinary boundaries, in both cultures in changing times.

Extinction Rebellion. 2019. *This Is Not a Drill: An Extinction Rebellion Handbook.* USA: Penguin Random House.

> Written by a polyphony of voices in the global activist movement, this slim volume is a handbook for lifestyle change and full of facts and stories to empower readers to take action on climate breakdown. Published in the wake of Greta Thunberg's campaign for environmental action, it's an example of the ongoing shift in public consciousness about the relationship between people and the planet.

Evans, Alex. 2017. *The Myth Gap: What Happens When Evidence and Arguments Aren't Enough?* UK: Transworld Publishers; USA: Penguin Random House.

> This little book challenges what counts as truth and how public arguments are developed. In reinvigorating the idea of myth in social discourse, Evans doesn't dismiss science and factual information, but he makes a compelling case for how stories can "bring us together and change the world."

Harington, C. Richard. 1968. *Denning Habits of the Polar Bear.* Canada: Canadian Wildlife Service Report Series, Number 5. Department of Indian and Northern Affairs.

A unique monograph based on five years of work done by zoologist Dick Harington while working as a Canadian Wildlife Service biologist. In mapping archival research onto his own empirical investigations of bear dens throughout the circumpolar world, Harington has produced a portrait of polar bear dens that stands as remarkable in its own right but also as a marker in time against which change can be measured and assessed.

Keith, Darren, with Jerry Arqviq, Louie Kamookak, Jackie Ameralik and the Gjoa Haven Hunters' and Trappers' Organization. 2005. Inuit Qaujimaningit Nanurnut/Inuit Knowledge of Polar Bears. Canada: Gjoa Haven Hunters' and Trappers' Organization and CCI Press (now Polynya Press, an imprint of the University of Alberta Press).

What I love about this book is that it is part of a growing literature of the north written and compiled by northerners for northerners and others interested in bear natural history, cultural significance, bear population dynamics, and Inuit hunting techniques. Published in both syllabic text and Roman orthography in Inuktitut and in English, this book has veracity and authenticity that put it on par with any research paper or scientific volume.

Keller, Evelyn Fox. 1983. *A Feeling for the Organism: The Life and Work of Barbara McClintock.* USA: W. H. Freeman & Company.

Although I veered away from biological inquiry into polar bears for more culturally based research in the 1970s, one my absolute heroes from science is Nobel Prize–winning plant geneticist Barbara McClintock. This beautifully crafted biography presents McClintock as a dogged and persistent investigator and a very broad and creative thinker when it came to the intricate secrets of the genetic organization of corn. Her courage not only in doing the work but also in dealing with the naysayers makes her an inspiring exemplar of how all disciplined inquiry should be done, for now and for the future.

MacDonald, John. 1998. *The Arctic Sky: Inuit Astronomy, Star Lore, and Legend.* Canada: Royal Ontario Museum/Nunavut Research Institute.

This is a wonderful and accessible volume about an Inuit perspective on the northern sky (which is very different from Greek or Roman takes on astronomy) that was researched with patience and respect. John MacDonald is a cultural anthropologist, but he is also a friend and collaborator for the many people around Igloolik, Nunavut, whose knowledge and stories enrich the pages of this remarkable book.

Nelson, Richard K. 1969. *Hunters of the Northern Ice.* USA/UK: the University of Chicago Press.

Richard K. Nelson, a wonderful writer and storyteller, takes an anthropological approach in this book, setting polar bears in a more cultural and ecological context drawn from his extensive time with the people of Wainwright, Alaska. His other works, like *Hunters of the Northern Forest* and *The Island Within,* also contain remarkable insights by this unsung nature writer.

Ovsyanikov, Nikita. 1996. *Polar Bears: Living with the White Bear.* USA: Voyageur Press.

I include this older volume not because of its natural history of the bear but because of its author. Nikita is one of the most captivating people I have met in more than forty years of Arctic travels. His accounts of polar bear behavior, based on living with them for months on end for several years on Wrangel Island, are fascinating. And while I disagree with some of his conclusions, particularly how subsistence hunting of polar bears by Indigenous peoples in North America is a driver of the global black market in polar bear products, he is a scientist who knows bears in a very different way from others in his field.

Phipps, Constantine John. 1775. *A Voyage Towards the North Pole: Undertaken by His Majesty's Command, 1773.* Ireland: James Williams.

In spite of the fact that Indigenous people worldwide have had their own nomenclature for every living thing since time immemorial, Western ways would have it that the honor of naming falls to the first scientist or observer who identifies an organism as a distinct species. In the case of the polar bear, that person was John Constantine Phipps on a voyage to the North Pole three quarters of the way through the eighteenth century. Through the wonders of the digital universe that increasingly envelops everything we do, Captain Phipps's record of that sighting is available in reproduction through a number of enterprising antiquarian online booksellers.

Stirling, Ian. 1990. *The Polar Bear.* UK: Blandford Press; USA: the University of Michigan Press.

There are many informative sources about the natural history and global population dynamics of polar bears, but the one I keep coming back to is this one. No one knows more about polar bears than Dr. Ian Stirling, and the text, along with the remarkable photography of Dan Guravich, make this book, available in libraries around the world, a classic. *Polar Bears: The Natural History of a Threatened Species* (2011) is an update of the original book and references large amounts of research, scientific material, and photographs published in the intervening twenty-one years. Stirling is also the lead author on a portrait of the early research done on Hudson Bay called "The Ecology of the Polar Bear (*Ursus Maritimus*) Along the Western Coast of Hudson Bay," in Canadian Wildlife Service *Occasional Paper* Number 33 (1977).

Trott, Christopher G. 2006. "The Gender of the Bear." *Études/ Inuit/Studies* 30(1): 89–109.

An absolutely fascinating and illuminating report on bears that draws on and contributes to Western anthropological scholarship by stretching conventional thinking in generative ways. Trott writes: "Inuit ethnology shows that there are clear boundaries between the animal and the human, the living and the dead, male and female, but also that each of these terms contains the other within it while simultaneously providing a passage between the two." Until an Inuit researcher engages the same questions and assumption, this paper is an important read.

Unger, Zac. 2013. *Never Look a Polar Bear in the Eye: A Family Field Trip to the Arctic's Edge in Search of Adventure, Truth, and Mini-Marshmallows.* USA: Da Capo Press, a member of the Perseus Books Group.

The next best thing to actually traveling to Churchill, Manitoba, known as "The Polar Bear Capital of the World," is to go there via the eyes and irreverent sensibilities of Californian firefighter-cum-writer Zac Unger. Engaging and illuminating, this book takes readers into the dog-eat-dog world of polar bear conservation politics.

Glossary

Aglu: An Inuktitut term referring to the breathing hole in sea ice that creates a cave or lair between ice and overlying snow in which seals breathe, give birth and nurse their young during the early stages of their development.

Auroras: Short for "aurora borealis," multicolored lights in the night sky, which occur in the earth's atmosphere, particularly in the north, when charged particles from the sun strike elements in the earth's upper atmosphere.

Beach ridge: A wave-created ridge of sorted sand and gravel running parallel to existing shorelines, it may be marooned or apparently moved inland by land that rises, having been released from the weight of past ice sheets.

Cellulase: An enzyme that allows some mammals to break down plant cellulose into usable sugars for digestion.

Chemical signature: A pattern visible through scientific analysis of compounds within an object or organism, something plants and animals have been reading forever as part of their life cycles with no external equipment at all.

Chuffing: A short puffing sound uttered by bears as a communication signal, often signaling uncertainty.

Conceptus: An embryo in a mammalian uterus, particularly in the early stages of pregnancy.

Equinox: The seasonal position of the earth relative to the sun reached on September 21 and March 21, when the sun is directly overhead at noon at the equator, creating exactly twelve hours of day and twelve hours of night everywhere on the planet.

Estuary: The tidal mouth of a large river where freshwater from the river and salt water from the ocean are intermixed by current and tide.

Floe: A sheet, or sheets, of floating, moving ice.

Global oceanic circulation: The process through which differences in salinity and temperature mix and cause ocean water and ice to move in predictable patterns.

Grid stake: A metal or wooden marker, often with signage or elevation marks, used to delimit areas of interest, such as those set out by mineral prospectors.

Guard hairs: The top or outer layer of hair in an animal's coat, generally longer and coarser than underlying, softer fur.

Gyre: Short for "ocean gyre," a large clockwise or counter-clockwise system of rotating ocean currents formed by wind and forces created by the earth's rotation.

Iglu: Also "igloo," an Inuktitut term describing a circular dome-shaped living space made of carved blocks of wind-hardened snow.

Keel: The submerged counterpart of an ice ridge.

Kingulliq: In Inuktitut, "the one behind" or "the last one." Kingulliq is also a star in the Inuit night sky, being the summer triangle star, Vega, in the European constellation Lyra.

Landfast ice: Ice, usually on the sea, that is attached to the shore.

Lead: A fracture within ice on sea or lake where the water is open.

Loft: A term, more often used in conjunction with winter coats or sleeping bags, to describe the thickness or amount of volume occupied by different insulating materials.

Mirage: An optical illusion caused by light being bent by atmospheric conditions, often visible over expanses of open land or sea ice.

Molted hair: Guard hairs and/or downy underfur that is shed to regulate an animal's body temperature and to make way for new growth.

Nanuq: Inuktitut for "polar bear."

Nanurjuk: Inuktitut term for a star known as "the bear-spirited one," often referring to the bright star known as Aldebaran in the European constellation Taurus.

Offal: Entrails or internal organs of animals that become food for another animal.

Pack ice: Expanses of pieces of floating ice, usually sea ice, driven together into a nearly solid mass by wind and currents.

PCBs: A group of human-made compounds called polychlorinated biphenyls, once used in heat transfer and hydraulic equipment, as pigments and dyes, and as plasticizers in paints and rubber products, banned since 1979 because of their toxicity but still present and doing damage to animals and ecosystems because of their persistence in living tissues.

Pressure ridge: An upwelling of sea ice, sometimes many dozens of yards high, produced on floating ice by the collision of two ice masses driven by water currents or winds.

Radiant heat: In contrast to heat transferred by conduction or convection, radiant heat is heat lost by an animal through electromagnetic waves.

Sassat: A Greenlandic Inuit term for a group of animals caught in the ice. In practice, on Hudson Bay, "sassat" describes a pond of open water in fast ice, far from the floe edge that supports the breathing of whales who have been trapped by rapidly advancing ice formation.

Sivulliq: In Inuktitut, "the first one" and part of the star cluster "Sivulliik" (the first ones), which is bright stars Arcturus and Muphrid in the European constellation Boötes.

Solstice: The seasonal position of the earth relative to the sun reached on June 21, when the sun is directly over the Tropic of Cancer, creating the longest day of the year in the northern hemisphere, and on December 21, when the sun is directly over the Tropic of Capricorn, creating the shortest day of the year in the northern hemisphere.

Stationary hunting: A practice of bears and humans that involves standing absolutely still for hours over a seal breathing hole, or aglu, until prey surfaces for air and is caught or harpooned by breaking through the dome of ice before the seal can escape back into the water.

Tussock tundra: Generally found on poorly drained clay soils over permafrost where clumps of vegetation build localized communities of grasses and related species that create a landscape of tussocks or sedge-topped "heads" sticking up in a matrix of unvegetated bare soils where water runs in warmer weather.

Vocalization: A sound uttered by an animal creating a communication lexicon; used by many species, including whales, bears, birds and beetles.

Wabusk: Cree language term for "polar bear."

Acknowledgments

Over forty years in the making, this book would not have come to be without Professor Keith Ronald, dean of biological sciences at the University of Guelph in the 1970s, who invited me into his lab and eventually asked me to wade in on a project to determine the spectral sensitivity of a polar bear nicknamed "Huxley." Even though in the fullness of time on that project, I turned away from marine biology toward more culturally situated learning—from studying bears to learning from the Indigenous people who know bears best—I must recognize and thank Dr. Ronald and Huxley for these indelible experiences.

Through the lifetime of travels and trails that led away from Zoology Annex III and the Laboratory Animal Building tucked in along Gordon Street behind the Veterinary College at the University of Guelph, many significant people have entered my world—hunters, elders, naturalists, researchers, teachers, mentors, friends, fellow travelers—each of whom, in a multiplicity of ways, contributed to learnings reflected in this book: among them—Robin Best, Lloyd Binder, Eddy Carmack, Arthur N. Chilingarov, Henry Ford, Keith Fraser, Geoff Green, Aleeasuk Idlout and Ozzie Kheraj, Arvaarluk Kusugak, Johnny Issaluk, Sergey Nikolayevich Kharyuchi, John Lee, Devon Manik, Venera Niyazova, Nikita Ovsyanikov, Angulalik Pedersen, Derek Pottle, David Serkoak, Vaycheslav Shadrin, Ed Struzik, Kenny Taptuna, Hugh and Ruth Tulurialik, and Kirk Wipper, to name but a few. Any deviations I have made from truths of your teachings are mine alone, but I thank you for sharing your wisdom.

For the impulse to explore a different approach to nonfictional storytelling, I must acknowledge creative collaborators—filmmakers mostly—like Goh Iromoto, Bill Mason, Joanne Page, Kathleen Shannon, and Jason van Bruggen, who showed me through their imaginative process, discipline, and workflow that there is no substitute for time spent in getting to know your subject and that emotional engagement happens best when a story is aimed first at the heart. And for the courage to explore the margins of creative nonfiction, and for bringing *Ice Walker* into the light, I must thank Kevin Hanson, Sarah St. Pierre and the wonderful editorial and production team at Simon & Schuster Canada, particularly my longtime friend and editor, Phyllis Bruce.

To Gail Simmons, my spouse and life partner of twoscore years, this one was different. Yes, you coddled, cajoled, read stuff, commented, critiqued, kept the home fires burning and carried on while this thirsty sack of contradictions was rambling in bear country and beyond for weeks, sometimes months, on end. But it was you who, through your fluency in the teachings of the energy world, held my hand on a path that led up eagle mountain and into the stillness, beauty and complexities of Nanu's essence, a learning journey that continues and yet without which this book in this form would never have come to be. Thank you. You have much to teach. I have much to learn, and I look forward to continuing adventures with you, even as we try to figure out together what grandparenting for a better future is all about.

Finally, to Mother Earth, I'm sorry. By better understanding the bear, we better understand ourselves. We can do better. We must do better. We are the bear, as my northern friends have known all along.

JR
Cranberry Lake
January 28, 2020

ICE
WALKER

James Raffan

—

This reading group guide for *Ice Walker* includes discussion questions and ideas for enhancing your book club. The suggested questions are intended to help your reading group find new and interesting angles and topics for your discussion. We hope that these ideas will enrich your conversation and increase your enjoyment of the book.

TOPICS AND QUESTIONS FOR DISCUSSION

1. How much did you know about the Arctic before reading this book? Does Nanu's story change your perception of life in the north and the plight of the polar bear?

2. What did you make of the author's argument that polar bears and polar peoples share an essential interconnection? How does Aisivak's story speak to this historic relationship?

3. The story is told primarily through Nanu's eyes. What effect did this have on you as you read the book?

4. The author chose not to make the bears talk. What senses does he invoke instead to convey how Nanu and her cubs experience the world around them?

5. How does the ice itself become a character in the story?

6. Consider the history of the land and the ice that Nanu instinctually knows, and discuss the role of memory in the book. What parallels might you draw between Nanu's memory and our own memory of human evolution and survival? How does this relate to the author's call to action in the final lines of the book?

7. How is climate change specifically affecting polar bears? How does the lack of ice affect hunting and migration patterns?

8. Leaving aside the man-made threats to the polar bears for a moment, were you surprised that, given all the natural dangers and obstacles they face, bears as a species are able to survive? What do you think this says about polar bears and life in the north?

9. At the heart of this story is a family. Were you worried for their safety? How did you feel when they were in danger?
10. What do you think happens to Kingu after the story ends?
11. What does "bearness" mean to you?
12. What is the significance of the title *Ice Walker*? Is there more than one ice walker in the book?
13. Besides the polar bear, who else's future in the north might be threatened? How has colonization and industrialization affected the Inuit way of life in the Arctic?
14. In recent years, we've seen an enormous shift toward environmental enlightenment with climate activists like Greta Thunberg. At present, do you think we've made strides in protecting our earth? Is there more to be done?

ENHANCE YOUR BOOK CLUB

1. To find out what you can do as an individual to combat climate change, visit the David Suzuki Foundation website and click "Take Action" to learn more. Check out the top ten things you can do about climate change here: https://davidsuzuki.org/what-you-can-do/top-10-ways-can-stop-climate-change/.

2. Visit Polar Bears International, an organization solely dedicated to wild polar bears and their conservation, and watch their live camera feeds of bears or follow bears as they journey across the ice via their bear tracker: http://polarbearsinternational.org/#polar-bear-cam.

3. To find out more about polar bears just like Nanu in the Canadian Arctic, go to the Polar Bears in Canada website: https://www.polarbearscanada.ca/en.

4. For more general information on polar bears, their natural history and conservation status, visit World Wildlife Fund at: https://www.worldwildlife.org/species/polar-bear.

5. Want to learn more? Here is a comprehensive and regularly updated bibliography of polar bear books and articles: http://ielc.libguides.com/sdzg/factsheets/polar bear/bibliography.

About the Author

Credit: Jason van Bruggen

Bestselling author and celebrated adventurer James Raffan has spent parts of each of the last forty-three years traveling, living and learning in the circumpolar world—in polar bear country. From the intensities of extended self-propelled expeditions by canoe, kayak, ski, snowshoe and on foot, to interminable waiting under wind-bound canvas for the Arctic weathers to change, to seeking out knowledge holders in the far corners of Siberia and beyond, to the relative comfort of being a lecturer and guide on ship-based Arctic journeys for adults and youth, he has probably covered more ground in more out-of-the-way places, by more means of locomotion, than almost any other traveler on earth. Over the years, James has written, edited and contributed to a variety of books on themes ranging from travel to field science, human geography and anthropology, with the connections between people and place as the common thread running through them all. He has also written for film, television and radio, both words and music, evoking the spirits and the stories of the confidants he has met along the way and campsites he has shared in faraway places. He has received numerous awards and recognitions, including being named one of Canada's most influential explorers of all time by *Canadian Geographic* in 2020; an honorary doctor of laws from the College of Biological Science at the University of Guelph; Canada's Meritorious Service Medal; and the Inuinnaqtun name "Aiuituk," conferred at a ceremony on the Coppermine River by the youth of Kugluktuk, Nunavut. With his wife, Gail Simmons, he divides home time between the Rideau Lakes of eastern Ontario on traditional Anishinaabe and Haudenosaunee territory and the Gulf Shore of Nova Scotia on traditional Mi'gma'gi ground.

www.jamesraffan.ca

 @raffjam